DESIGN
BASICS

Cover: "Two Roses," by David Holt

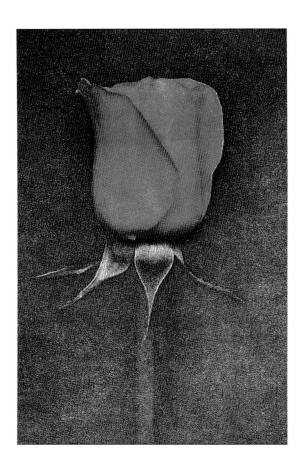

DAVID A. LAUER

College of Alameda, Alameda, California

THIRD EDITION

DESIGN
BASICS

Holt, Rinehart and Winston, Inc.

FT. WORTH • CHICAGO • SAN FRANCISCO
PHILADELPHIA • MONTREAL • TORONTO
LONDON • SYDNEY • TOKYO

for Eleanor

PUBLISHER Charlyce Jones Owen

ACQUISITIONS EDITOR Janet Wilhite

PICTURE RESEARCHER Elsa Peterson

PRODUCTION MANAGEMENT York Production Services

PRODUCTION/MANUFACTURING COORDINATOR Kathleen Ferguson

COMPOSITION AND COLOR York Graphic Services

PRINTING AND BINDING R. R. Donnelley & Sons

Library of Congress Cataloging in Publication Data
Lauer, David A.
    Design basics / David A. Lauer. — 3rd ed.
        p.   cm.
    Includes bibliographical references.
    ISBN 0-03-030422-9
    1. Design.   I. Title.
NK 1510.L38   1990   89-26731
745.4—dc20   CIP

Address Editorial Correspondence to: 301 Commerce Street, Suite 3700, Fort Worth, TX 76102

Address Orders to: 6277 Sea Harbor Drive, Orlando, FL 32887
1-800-782-4479, or 1-800-433-0001 (in Florida)

Printed in the United States of America

0 1 2   039 9 8 7 6 5 4 3 2

Holt, Rinehart and Winston
The Dryden Press
Saunders College Publishing

PREFACE

A survey was taken a few years ago of college Design instructors and their attitudes about textbooks. In answer to one of the questions, some 60 percent of the instructors said the available textbooks were "structured differently" from their course. This is hardly a surprising fact. Probably no two design courses in this country are taught the same way—nor should they be. Many of us don't even teach the Design class in the same way in successive school terms.

This wide diversity in approach is exactly the reason *Design Basics* was initially conceived in a modular format. The purpose of putting the information into self-contained units was to allow individual instructors to use it in any sequence that fitted their purpose. No particular order was "built in" for either casual reading or classroom use.

Another question on the survey elicited the response that instructors wanted design topics covered "in more depth." This again is not an unusual or unexpected response. However, any textbook on whatever subject can only begin to cover a field of study. Naturally, this book is not all-inclusive, as shelves of library books dealing with the many individual topics can attest. This text attempts (as the title suggests) to be a *basic* introduction to a vast array of visual ideas.

Several changes in this third edition will be immediately apparent. The chapter on problem solving or finding visual solutions to design problems has been expanded and moved to the first of the text. The material on value (previously included in the color chapter) has been developed into a separate chapter. The color chapter now includes new topics and hence more color reproductions. This chapter is now the last chapter in the book—a position that seems helpful when the aspect of color is taught in a separate course.

More small charts or diagrams now exist to illustrate the various concepts in a basic, non-objective manner. In addition, *all* of these charts have been redesigned in a crisper, sharper style. Since these charts are often mentioned as definite teaching/learning tools, the changes should be helpful.

Other changes are less obvious. Many sections have been reorganized, and several chapters include new topics. Of course, there are many new illustrations (almost half of the pictures are changed), and these have continued to maintain the same varied mix of media, periods, styles, geography, and so on. Techniques, materials, and purposes vary widely, but the same basic guidelines and practices apply to all the fields in the visual arts. It is hoped that this book can be an introduction for students no matter what may be their particular career or personal aims.

This revision has attempted to retain the positive features of the first editions, while adding new elements. The writing continues to try to present these topics in clear, easily understood language. However, as Somerset Maugham said: "There are three rules for writing well. Unfortunately no one knows what they are."

ACKNOWLEDGMENTS

So many people assist, directly and indirectly, in the process of writing a book. I wish to especially thank Ernest B. Ball and James E. Jewell for specific help and constant encouragement. The reviewers who thoughtfully considered endless pages of material and made so many good suggestions are certainly to be thanked:

William A. Marriott, *The University of Georgia*
Richard A. Niewerth, *Anne Arundel Community College*
Jack Mann, *Wittenberg University*
Crit Streed, *University of Northern Iowa*
Barbara E. Meyer, *Northwood Institute*
Harriette C. F. Laskin, *Tidewater Community College*
Patrick J. Shuck, *Meramec Community College*
Joy Dohr, *University of Wisconsin*

CONTENTS

CONTENTS

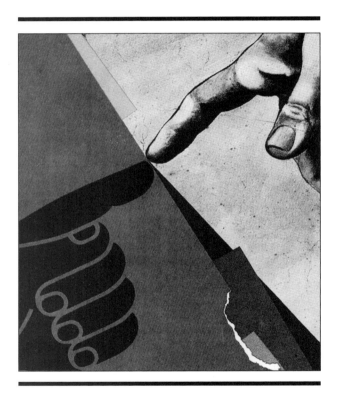

DESIGN PROBLEM SOLVING

Introduction

Graphic design. Interior design. Industrial design. Package design. Architectural design. Theatrical design. Fashion design. Lighting design . . . .

All these varied areas (and many more) use the word "design." Thousands of artists working in these very diverse fields are called "designers." What do these fields have in common?

Design is the planned arrangement of elements to form a visual pattern. Depending on the field, these "elements" will vary—all the way from painted symbols to written words to windows or furniture. But the result in each case is always a *visual* organization. To *design* means to *plan,* to *organize* **(a).** Design is essentially the opposite of chance. In ordinary conversation, when we say "it happened by design" we mean something was planned and did not occur just by accident. Of course, people in all occupations plan, but the artist or designer plans something that other people will *look at* and observe. Art, like other careers and occupations, is concerned with seeking answers to problems. Art differs only in that its answers are visual solutions.

The arts are called "creative" fields because there are no predetermined correct answers to the problems. Infinite variations in individual interpretation and application are possible. Problems in art vary in specifics and complexity and take various forms. Independent painters or sculptors usually create their own problems or avenues they wish to explore. These may be as wide or as narrow as the artist chooses. The architect or graphic and industrial designer is usually *given* the problem, often with very specific options and clearly defined limitations. Students in art classes also usually are in this category—they execute a series of assignments devised by the instructor and requiring rather specific solutions. However, all art or visual problems are similar in that a creative solution is desired.

We use the word "creative" to mean a solution that is original, imaginative, fresh, or unusual. The creative aspect of art is effectively expressed in **b.** Taking a cue from Michelangelo's famous *Creation of Adam* fresco on the Sistine ceiling, the designer visually symbolizes, in a very simple manner, this creativity of both fine artists and graphic designers. To be creative is a challenge, but many of us are creative in some area. Now this ability must be applied to the visual arts.

The creative aspect of art also includes the often-heard phrase that "there are no rules in art." This is true. In solving visual problems, there is no list of strict or absolute *dos* and *don'ts* to follow. Given all the varied objectives of visual art through the ages, definite laws are impossible. However, the "no rules" phrase may seem to imply that all designs are equally valid and visually successful. This is not true. Artistic practices and criteria have been developed from successful works, of which an artist or designer should be aware. Thus, guidelines (*not* rules) exist that usually will assist in the creation of successful designs. These guidelines certainly do not mean that the artist is limited to any specific solution.

Discussions of art often distinguish between two aspects, *content* and *form*. *Content* implies the subject matter, story, or information that the artwork seeks to communicate to the viewer. *Form* is the purely visual aspect, the manipulation of the various elements and principles of design. Content is what artists want to say, form is how they say it. Problems in art can concern one or both categories.

Sometimes the aim of a work of art is purely aesthetic. Subject matter can be absent and the problem related only to creating visual pleasure. Purely abstract adornment or decoration is a very legitimate role in art. Very often, however, problems in art have a purpose beyond mere visual satisfaction. Art is, and always has been, a means of communication.

---

a *It's Time to Get Organized.* 1986. Poster. John Kuchera, Art Director and Designer; Hutchins/Y&R.

b *Connections.* 1986. Poster for Simpson Paper Co. James Cross, Art Director; Ken Parkhurst, Designer; Cross Associates.

a

b

CONNECTIONS

Ken Parkhurst

Introduction

We have all heard the cliché "a picture is worth a thousand words." This is true. There is no way to calculate how much each of us has learned through pictures. Communication has always been an essential role for art. Written communication indeed can be traced back to when "writing" was done simply in pictorial symbols rather than letters. Today, pictures can function as a sort of international language. A picture can be understood when written words may be unintelligible to the foreigner or the nonliterate. We do not need to understand German to grasp immediately that the message of the poster in **a** is pain, suffering, and torture.

In art as communication, the artist or designer is *saying* something to the viewer. Here the successful solution not only is visually effective but also communicates an idea. Any of the elements of art can be used in communication. Purely abstract lines, colors, and shapes can be very effective in expressing ideas or feelings. Many times the communication is achieved through symbols, pictorial images that suggest to the viewer the theme or message. The ingenuity or creative imagination exercised in selecting these images can be important in the finished work's success.

In art as communication, images are frequently combined with written words. The advertisements we see every day usually use both elements, coordinated to reinforce the design's purpose. Countless paintings demonstrate that words are not a necessity for communication. Three examples are shown that all suggest the idea of movement or change. In *Dog on a Leash* **(b)** we instantly feel the motion taking place. No words are needed to communicate the idea. The same is true of the design in **c.** Here though, the printed copy adds the specific information that the art design studio has moved its offices to a new location. In the third example **(d)** the two approaches are combined. Now, intellectually we read the word, but the visual presentation also conveys the basic idea of movement immediately.

These successful design solutions are due, of course, to good ideas. "How do I get an idea?" is a question often heard from students. Actually, almost everyone shares this dilemma from time to time. Even the professional artist can stare at the empty canvas, the successful writer at the blank page in the typewriter. An idea in art can take many forms, varying from a specific visual effect to an intellectual communication of a definite message. Ideas encompass both the areas of content and form.

It is doubtful that anyone can truly explain why or how an idea suddenly arises. While doing one thing, we can be thinking about something else. Our ideas can occur when we are in the shower, mowing the lawn, or in countless other seemingly unlikely situations. An answer to what we have been puzzling over can appear "out of the blue." But we need not be concerned here with sudden solutions. They will continue to happen, but is that the only procedure? The relevant question is, "What can we do consciously to stimulate this creative process?" What sort of activities can promote the likelihood that a solution to a problem will present itself?

Many people today are concerned with such questions. There has been a great deal of study of the "creative process," and a number of worthwhile books and articles have been devoted to it, featuring numerous technical terms to describe aspects of this admittedly complex subject. But let me suggest three very simple activities with very simple names:

Thinking
Looking
Doing

These activities are *not* sequential steps and certainly not independent procedures. They overlap and may be accomplished almost simultaneously or by jumping back and forth from one to another. Individuals vary; people are not programmed machines in which rigid step-by-step procedures lead inevitably to answers; people's feelings and intuitions may assist in making decisions. Problems vary so that a specific assignment may immediately suggest an initial emphasis on one of these suggestions. But all three procedures can stimulate the artistic problem-solving process.

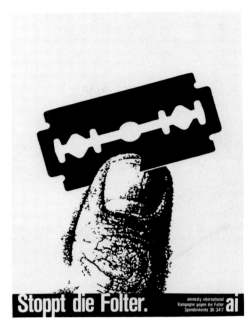

a

b

a *Stop Torture.* 1985. Poster for Amnesty International. Stephan Bundi,
Art Director and Designer; Atelier Bundi, Bern, Switzerland.

b Giacomo Balla. *Dynamism of a Dog on a Leash.* 1912. Oil on canvas,
35⅜ × 43¼″ (90 × 110 cm). Albright-Knox Art Gallery, Buffalo, New
York (Bequest of A. Conger Goodyear and George F. Goodyear, 1964).

c *Moving to Serve You Better.* 1986. Poster. John Kjos, Art Director; David
Clune, Designer; Ampersand Studios, Inc., Denver.

d The graphic technique matches the word's meaning to convey the idea.

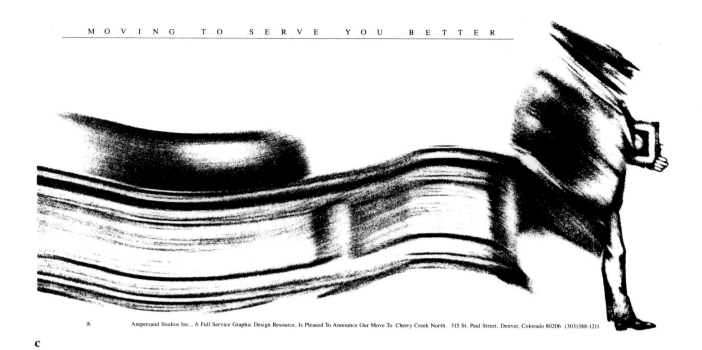

&   Ampersand Studios Inc., A Full Service Graphic Design Resource, Is Pleased To Announce Our Move To Cherry Creek North. 315 St. Paul Street, Denver, Colorado 80206 (303)388-1211

c

d

Procedures

THINKING

Georges Braque, the well-known French artist, wrote in his *Cahiers* (notebooks) that "one must not *think up* a picture." His point is valid; a painting is often a long process that should not be forced or created by formula to order. However, each day countless designers must indeed "think up" solutions to design problems; *thinking* is an essential part of this solution. When confronted by a problem in any aspect of life, the usual first step is to think about it. This is applicable also to art and visual problems. Thinking is involved in all aspects of the creative process. Every step in creating a design involves choices, and the selections are determined by thinking. Chance or accident is also an element in art. But art cannot be created mindlessly, although some twentieth-century art movements have attempted to eliminate rational thought as a factor in creating art and to stress intuitive or subconscious thought. But even then it is thinking that decides whether the spontaneously created result is worthwhile or acceptable. To say that "thinking" is somehow outside the artistic process is truly impossible.

Knowing what you are doing must precede your doing it. So thinking starts with understanding the problem at hand:

Precisely what is to be achieved? (What specific visual and/or intellectual effect is desired?)

Are there visual stylistic requirements (illustrative, abstraction, nonobjective, etc.)?

What physical limitations (size, color, media, etc.) are imposed?

When is the solution needed?

These questions may all seem self-evident, but effort spent on solutions outside the range of these specifications will not be productive. "Failures" can occur simply because the problem was not fully understood at the very beginning.

Thinking can be especially important in art that has a specific theme or message. How can the concept be communicated in visual terms? A first step is to think logically of which images or pictures could represent this theme and to list them or, better yet, sketch them quickly, since a visual answer is what you're seeking. Let's take a specific example: What could visually represent the idea of art or design? Some obvious symbols are shown in **a,** and you quickly will think of more. You might expand the idea by discussing it with others. They may offer suggestions you have not considered. Professional designers often are assisted by reports from market surveys that reveal the ideas of vast numbers of people.

Sketch your ideas to see immediately the visual potential. At this point you do not necessarily decide on *one* idea. But it's better to narrow a broad list to a few ideas worthy of development. Choosing a visual symbol is only the first step. How is the symbol to be used? Of course, countless possibilities exist. The examples in **b** and **c** use the common pencil to represent the idea of design. But these solutions are very different, and both are imaginative. In **b** the pencil is a "plow" cultivating a crop of artistic flowers at the right. The Rembrandtlike portrait in **c** features unexpectedly a pencil thrust through the subject's nose (like the familiar image of an aborigine with a bone in his nose). The startling juxtaposition of seemingly unrelated images is arresting.

Selecting a particular symbol may depend on limitations of size, medium, color, and so on. Even thinking of the future viewers may be an influence. To whom is this visual message addressed? What reaction do you want from this audience? What effect or feeling do you wish to create? To symbolize *art* as a bearded figure in a spattered smock and beret could be humorously effective in some situations while silly or trivial in others. Neither of the wonderful illustrations in **b** and **c** would be appropriate for the cover of any erudite book on aesthetics.

a Some visual symbols for art and design immediately come to mind.
b *Open House at Art Center.* 1988. Poster invitation for Art Center, Pasadena. Richard Louderback, Designer.
c Joel Peter Johnson. Cover design for *Print* magazine. September/October 1987.

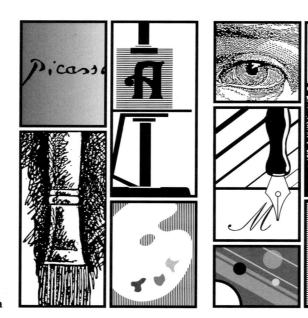

a

b

c

Procedures

LOOKING

Looking is probably the primary education of any artist. An often-heard truism states that "nature is the artist's teacher." Perhaps. Nature often may be the artist's *inspiration*. But the artist learns more by observing other art. Studying art from all periods and regions is enlightening. The more familiar you are with how other artists have solved various visual problems, the better equipped you will be to find your own solution. Artists cannot work in a vacuum; they are concerned with, and influenced by, the past and contemporary works of others. Our advantage today (unlike the past) is that so much visual information is readily accessible through newspapers, books, and magazines. It is relatively easy for us to see how diverse artists from all geographic areas are working.

Looking can be a part of any other activity. Whatever you are doing—walking down the street looking in store windows, leafing through a new magazine, selecting purchases in a store, visiting a local gallery, discussing student projects in class—*look* by analyzing what you see. When your attention is captured by an effective or dramatic visual image, try to figure out why. Why has a certain design (or arrangement) attracted your attention? How is this achieved? The particular subject matter, medium, or artist should be irrelevant—you are looking for basic visual concepts, concepts you can then adapt to your own purposes, subject, or theme. For example, look at the accompanying illustrations. They are all effective designs. Their subject matter, media, and immediate purposes are varied. Yet they are similar in that all use a similar design device: In each design, major elements are abruptly cut off by the edges of the format. Our attention is caught by this very unusual placement, so different from what we expect to see. In **a** and **b,** human figures are drastically truncated by the borders. In **c** the large piano shape on the right unites several smaller elements. But many of these, including lettered titles, are abruptly cut off on the right edge. The visual effect is not only surprising, but gives a very informal (almost accidental) feeling to the composition.

A good practice is to make a quick sketch to serve as a note of a design that seems to have a unique idea, either through symbol or visual pattern. Many artists keep clippings of effective designs in a "scrap file" to refer to for possible inspiration on future assignments.

This book is filled with illustrations showing visual ideas. Of course, one does not *copy* or slavishly imitate another artist's work and your work will not be identical to any of these examples. These illustrations provide raw material from which you may fashion a new and original idea. Ideas for a new machine or invention are protected by a patent, but this is not true of visual ideas. In this field, everyone learns from the successes (and failures) of other artists. The more you can observe and develop your critical judgment, the better it will serve you in future problem solving.

This all describes *looking* in a general sense. Looking also includes the more formal aspect of *research*. Some projects may involve subjects about which you have little knowledge or experience. Then visual research in books or magazines limited to the specific topic will not only be helpful but necessary.

---

a Andō Hiroshige. *The Benten Shrine Seen from Haneda Ferry.* From *One Hundred Famous Views of Edo.* 1856–58. Color woodcut. 13⅞ × 9½" (35.3 × 24 cm). Museum für Ostasiatische Kunst, Cologne.

b *Celebrating the Golden Summer of 1984.* 1984. Poster for the *New York Times.* Peter Schaefer, Art Director and Designer; Ken Joudrey, Artist.

c Signature promotion for Mead Paper. 1987. Mark Stockstill/Graphica Miamisburg, Designer; Mike Bonilla, Mark Stockstill and Nick Stamas, Illustrators.

a

Celebrating the Golden Summer of 1984
The New York Times

b

c

Procedures

DOING

Doing may seem like a needless suggestion, as most art eventually involves the act of creating the finished project. The exception is a *conceptual art* piece, where the process can stress thinking mainly. But this is unusual. Since art is a visual field, thinking, talking, and looking constitute only the initial steps of the creative process. For example, in creating a collage such as **a,** a general approach or visual effect may be thought out beforehand. But, the actual design can result only from moving and arranging the elements and seeing the results. To a greater or lesser extent, this is true of all design solutions.

What *doing* means here is to start experimenting visually, even if you have no clear direction in mind. If you are dealing with a purely visual problem (no theme, message, subject matter), then your visual experimenting should start immediately. Even with more complex problems involving concepts and symbols, actually *doing* something can stimulate the thinking aspect. Actually *seeing* your experiments may suggest other possibilities to you. A series of spontaneous, quickly done ''roughs'' (almost like a visual brainstorming) can be very helpful in helping you decide a direction to pursue.

Sometimes artists themselves cannot tell you what exact procedure or technique gave them the solution. The trademark designs in **b** and **c** are solutions that could well have come from a visual ''playing'' with possibilities.

The design in **b** is a logo to symbolize the twenty-fifth anniversary of the UCLA Department of Fine Arts. Because mere *thinking* of the numerals 2 and 5 would not seem to suggest a human figure, this marvelous dual-image design probably came about through repeated experimental sketches.

Trademark **(c)** was designed for a trucking firm. The sloping slides of the capital letter A (the company's initial) could have visually reminded the artist of a highway seen in perspective, and a very effective design resulted.

Students often look concerned and say, ''I don't know what I'm doing.'' This is not usually a problem or a cause for worry. They are experimenting visually, and as long as they are alert to what might

(or might not) develop, the process can be extremely useful. Great designs have evolved from almost unconscious doodling.

In this entire process of creating a design, experimentation is paramount. Do not settle for the first reasonable answer. Try lots of possibilities and variations, even if you eventually reject them all and return to your first idea. Of course, time limitations can be important, but the exploration is time well spent. Your decision is now based on a choice from many possibilities, not just one or two.

Independent artists may arrive at solutions on their own time schedule; in the many fields of applied art, ''deadlines'' are an unhappy fact of life. Usually in the business world, only so much time can be allotted to this act of creation. Artists in these fields accept this and must budget their time accordingly. A late class project is very serious; a late project at work can cost you money or a job.

Once you have decided on a basic idea or direction, the *doing* is the primary consideration. Ideas are developed through a series of rough, rather quickly done sketches that explore various, now purely visual, solutions. Needless to say, *thinking* is still involved as you select and choose, and your previous *looking* can suggest further design possibilities. The time involved in the visual development of an idea varies from problem to problem. But very often it is helpful to get reactions—whether from a client or an instructor or even friends—during the early stages.

Art is basically visual invention—*inventing* a creative solution to a visual problem. This design process has been nicely expressed by Josef Albers:

> *To design is*
> *to plan and organize*
> *to order and relate*
> *and to control.*
> *In short it embraces*
> *all means opposing*
> *disorder and accident.*
> *Therefore it signifies*
> *a human need*
> *and qualifies man's*
> *thinking and doing.*

a

b

TWENTY-FIVE YEARS OF THE ARTS
UCLA COLLEGE OF FINE ARTS

c

a Kurt Schwitters. *From Kate Steinitz.* 1945. Collage, 13¼ × 10¼"
(33 × 26 cm). Courtesy Marlborough Fine Art Ltd., London.
b Logo for UCLA College of Fine Arts. 1985. John Coy, Art Director and
Designer; Coy, Los Angeles.
c Trademark for Adams Trucking. Eric Bloom, Designer; Pairadice Design,
Santa Cruz, CA.

C H A P T E R

UNITY

a

b

Introduction

Unity, the presentation of a unified image, is perhaps as close to a ''rule'' as art can approach. Unity means that a congruity or agreement exists among the elements in a design; they *look* as though they belong together, as though some visual connection beyond mere chance has caused them to come together. Another term for the same idea is *harmony*. If the various elements are not harmonious, if they appear separate or unrelated, your pattern falls apart and lacks unity.

Example **a** illustrates the idea. When we look at the elements in this design, we immediately see that they are all somewhat similar. Despite obvious differences, they all have some basic visual characteristics that tend to relate them to each other. This harmony or unity is not merely from our recognizing all these items as ''bottles.'' If we had never before seen bottles, knew nothing of the uses for these containers, or even had no name for these glass objects, we would still see the *visual* similarity between them all. They are related *visually* because of some basic similarities in shape, and this provides a concept of unity.

The same subject is used in **b,** now an artist's pen-and-ink drawing. Again the unity results from our feeling of a relationship among the shapes as well as a similarity of linear shading on the various forms.

The relief sculpture in **c** shows this same idea in abstract terms, using shapes that have no literal meaning to the viewer. In looking at the three panels, we quickly recognize that all of them contain the same half-circle shapes. As with the bottles, different sizes are obvious, but the shape remains consistent.

The arrangement of these elements varies in each panel, but our sensing the similarity of shapes relates the three together in a coherent pattern. As the title of the sculpture states, an underlying *theme* is presented in several different ways as *variations*. This is the essence of the concept of unity.

The unity of a design is planned and controlled by the artist. Sometimes it stems naturally from the elements chosen, as in these examples. But, more often it reflects the skill of the designer to create a unified pattern from varied elements. Another term for ''design'' is the word *composition*, which implies the same feeling of organization. Just as a ''composition'' in an English class is not merely a haphazard collection of words and punctuation marks, so a visual composition is not a careless scattering of random items around a format.

a The units of this design have characteristics in common, despite obvious differences in appearance.

b Marcia Milner. *Still Life with Wine Bottle.* 1978. Pen and ink, 7⅝ × 10¾" (19.4 × 27.3 cm).

c Barbara Hepworth. *Maquette, Theme and Variations.* 1970. Bronze, 11⅜ × 16⅛" (29 × 66 cm). Private collection.

c

a

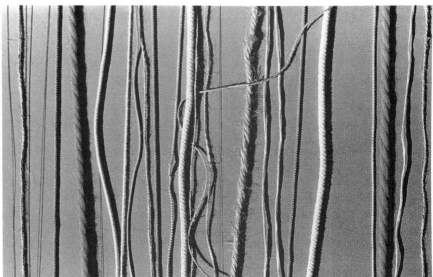

b

Introduction

An important aspect of visual unity is that the whole must be predominant over the parts; you must first see the *whole* pattern before you notice the individual elements. Each item may have a meaning and certainly add to the total effect, but the viewer must first see the pattern as a whole, rather than merely a collection of bits and pieces.

This concept differentiates a design from the usual scrapbook page. In a scrapbook, each item is meant to be observed and studied individually, to be enjoyed and then forgotten as your eye moves on to the next souvenir. The result may be interesting, but is not a unified design.

The collage in **a** is a design. It is similar to a scrapbook in that it contains many diverse elements, but we are aware first of the total pattern they make together, and then we begin to enjoy the items separately.

Do not confuse *intellectual unity* with *visual unity*. Visual unity denotes some harmony or agreement between the items that is apparent to the *eye*. To say that a scrapbook page is "unified" because all the items have a common theme (your family, your wedding, your vacation at the beach) is unity of *idea*—that is, a conceptual unity not observable by the eye.

A unifying *idea* will not necessarily produce a unified pattern. The fact that all the elements in **a** deal with Black History is interesting but irrelevant to the visual organization.

The unity in **b** does not derive from our recognizing all the items in the design as bits of rope, string, thread, and so on. The visual unity stems from the repetition of tall, linear, vertical elements. Then the varying weights and colors in an irregular spatial pattern add interest.

The need for visual unity does not deny that very often there is also an intellectual pleasure in design. Many times the task of a designer is to convey an idea or theme. Now the visual unity function is important along with an intellectual "reading" of the design. One example can show this dual appreciation. The advertisement in **c** shows immediate visual unity as we see three rows of varied, but very similar, shapes lined up both horizontally and vertically. Then intellectually we recognize that in the bottom row, one shape is indeed not a butterfly, but a *farfalle* or butterfly-shaped Italian pasta. The surprise recognition of something to eat amid a similar pattern of insects is delightful.

---

a Collage for *National Geographic* magazine. January 1988. Fred Otnes, Designer. © National Geographic Society.

b We don't need to know what the items are to see the visual similarity of tall, slender verticals.

c *Farfalle from Barilla. If You Want to Catch Them, You Have to Put Parmesan Cheese on Their Tails.* 1987. Jean-Claude Jouis, Art Director; Gilbert Scher, Copywriter; Paul Goirand, Photographer; TBWA, Paris.

c

Gestalt

The designer's job in creating a visual unity is made easier by the fact that the viewer is actually *looking* for some sort of organization, something to relate the various elements. The viewer does not *want* to see confusion or unrelated chaos. The designer must provide some clues, but the viewer is already attempting to find some coherent pattern and unity. Indeed, when such a pattern cannot be found, it seems the viewer will turn away and simply ignore the image.

This is one of the conclusions that studies in the area of perception have shown. Since early in this century, psychologists have done a great deal of research on visual perception, attempting to discover just how the eye and brain function together. Much of this research is, of course, very technical and scientific. The artist or designer can find it useful to understand some of the basic findings. The most widely known of these perception studies is called the *gestalt* theory of visual psychology.

Look at a few very simple and elementary concepts that only begin to suggest the range of these studies and their conclusions:

The viewer tends to *group* objects that are close to each other into a larger unit. Therefore, our first impression of **a** is not merely some random squares, but two groups of smaller elements.

Negative (or empty) spaces will likewise be organized. In **b** the many elements immediately are seen as two groups. However, with all the shapes ending on two common boundaries, the impression of the slanted white diagonal shape is as strong as the various rectangles.

Our brain will tend to relate and group objects of a similar shape. Hence in **c** a cross or *plus* sign is obvious rather than an all-over pattern of small shapes.

In **d** the pattern is not merely many circles of various sizes. Instead we will *close* the spaces between similar ones to form a design of "lines." These diagonal "lines" organize themselves to give the impression of an *M* shape.

The list of examples could go on and on.

The tower in **e** was constructed for the Olympic Games in Los Angeles. It is a very complicated visual pattern involving letters, colored panels, stars, numbers, circles, and so forth. This complexity, of course, described the event itself, with thousands of athletes from all over the world competing in hundreds of different events. As we look at this tower, we are aware of this exciting diversity of elements. But quickly we also see the constant repetition of squares with their *X*-shaped supports made by the aluminum scaffolding. Then, notice how all the other elements are visually related to this basic framework. Now the whole design seems organized and "tied" together. Our brain looks for similar elements, and when we recognize them we see a cohesive design rather than unorganized chaos.

a We instantly see two groups of shapes.
b The white diagonal is as obvious as are the two groups of rectangles.
c Grouping similar shapes makes us see a plus sign in the center.
d The circles seem to form "lines," and we see an *M*-shape.
e Tower for the Olympic Games, Los Angeles, 1984.

a

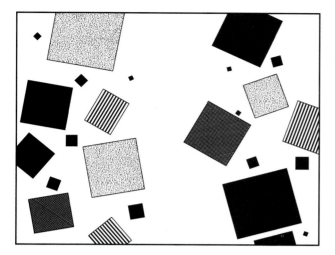

b

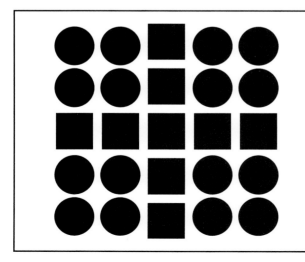

c

d

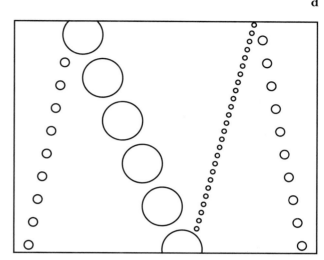

e

c

d

Ways to Achieve Unity

PROXIMITY

An easy way to gain unity—to make separate elements look as if they belong together—is by *proximity*, simply putting these elements close together. The four elements in **a** appear isolated, as floating bits with no relationship to each other. By putting them close together **(b),** we begin to see them as a total, related pattern. Proximity is a common unifying factor. Through proximity we recognize constellations in the skies and, in fact, are able to read. Change the proximity scheme that makes letters into words, and reading becomes impossible.

The painting by Thomas P. Anshutz **(c)** of workers on their lunch break shows the idea in composition. The lighter elements of the workers' half-stripped bodies contrast with the generally darker background. However, these light elements are not placed aimlessly around the composition but, by proximity, are arranged carefully to unite visually. Arms stretch and reach out to touch or overlap adjoining figures so the bodies form a large horizontal unit stretching across the painting.

Paul Wonner's painting **(d)** is an interesting collection of still life objects that are essentially isolated from each other. But notice how the very careful placement and the strategic use of shadows visually tie the elements together by proximity. Our eyes move smoothly from one item to the next.

Proximity is the simplest way to achieve unity, and many artworks employ this technique. Without proximity (with largely isolated elements), the artist must put greater stress on the other methods to unify an image.

---

a If they are isolated from one another, elements appear unrelated.
b Placing items close together makes us see them first as a group.
c Thomas P. Anshutz. *The Ironworkers' Noontime.* 1880. Oil on canvas, 17 × 24″ (43.2 × 61 cm). M.H. De Young Memorial Museum. The Fine Arts Museums of San Francisco.
d Paul Wonner. *Dutch Still Life with Stuffed Birds and Chocolates,* detail. 1981. Acrylic on canvas, 6 × 4′ (1.8 × 1.22 m). Collection Harry Cohn, Hillsborough, CA.

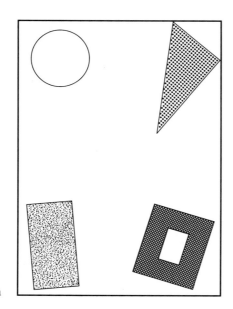

a

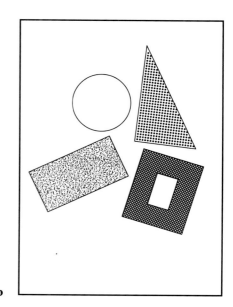

b

Ways to Achieve Unity

REPETITION

A most valuable and widely used device for achieving visual unity is *repetition*. As the term implies, something simply repeats in various parts of the design to relate the parts to each other. The element that repeats may be almost anything—a color, a shape, a texture, a direction, or an angle. In the painting by Kupka **(a)**, composition is based solely on one shape: circles and arcs, or segments of circles. These slightly diffused circular elements are of different sizes and varying tones, and they overlap in a nonconcentric pattern, sometimes opaque and sometimes transparent to show the form behind (or in front?). But the repetition of just one shape can create an interesting composition.

Louise Nevelson's sculpture **(b)** also shows unity by repetition. The complicated pattern of small fragments of wood over the whole surface is a unifying element in itself, almost reminiscent of a Gothic cathedral's intricate facade. But another factor of visual unity is the frequent repetition of vertical rectangular boxes, each one enclosing and framing varying patterns of small details. The repetition of these larger shapes welds the entire pattern into a coherent composition.

Similarly, in naturalistic art with subject matter, repetition can be a unifying factor. In Degas' *The Millinery Shop* **(c)**, notice how often the artist repeats a circle motif. Just as in **a**, circles are a repeating element of visual unity, but now the circles represent objects such as hats, flowers, bows, the woman's head, bosom, and skirt, and so forth. The painting is a whole design of circles broken by a few verticals (the hat stand, the ribbons, the back draperies) and a triangle or so (the table, the woman's bent arm, and the front hat's ribbons). When we look beyond the subject matter in art, we begin to recognize the artist's use of repetition to create a sense of unity.

In paintings or designs with color, it can be an immediate way to create unity.

SEE ALSO: RHYTHM, PAGES 93 TO 103.

a Frantisek Kupka. *Disks of Newton.* 1912. Oil on canvas, 39½ × 29″ (101 × 74 cm). Philadelphia Museum of Art (Louise and Walter Arensberg Collection).

b Louise Nevelson. *Tide I, Tide.* 1963. Wood, approx. 9 × 12′ (2.74 × 3.66 m). Collection Mr. and Mrs. Albert List, Byram, CT.

c Edgar Degas. *The Millinery Shop.* 1879–1884. Oil on canvas, 39⅛ × 43⅜″ (100 × 110.7 cm). © 1989 The Art Institute of Chicago (Mr. and Mrs. Lewis Larned Coburn Memorial Collection). All rights reserved.

a

b

c

Ways to Achieve Unity

CONTINUATION

A third way to achieve unity is by *continuation*, a more subtle device than proximity or repetition, which are fairly obvious. Continuation, naturally, means that something "continues"—usually a line, an edge, or a direction from one form to another. The viewer's eye is carried smoothly from one to the next.

The design in **a** is unified by the closeness and the character of the elements. In **b** though, the shapes seem even more of a unit, since they are arranged in such a way that one's vision flows easily from one element to the next. The shapes no longer float casually. They are now organized into a definite, set pattern.

Human figures, animals, plants, and a ship are drawn in whimsical abstract form in Picasso's painting **(c).** Notice how the majority of these shapes share an edge with two strong wavy, horizontal lines extending across the canvas. This visually unites the forms.

The pastel drawing by Degas **(d)** is much more naturalistic with the forms quite representational. But the same use of continuation can be seen as the eye is carried from one form to another by placement. The line of the round tub starts at the bather's hairline, meets her fingertips, and joins the vertical line of the shelf where the brush handle overlaps. The circular shape of the bather's hips is tangential to the same shelf edge. Notice the careful arrangement of the objects on the shelf—how each item barely touches or carries the eye to another. That at first glance the arrangement seemed casual and unplanned only adds to our admiration of the artist.

Continuation is the standard device employed by graphic designers planning layouts for books, magazine editorial pages, advertisements, brochures, and so on. In each case the artist must somehow create a sense of visual unity from the very disparate elements of printed headlines, blocks of copy, photographs, and trademarks. Lining up various shapes with a continuation of edges **(e)** is the most practical and satisfactory solution.

a Proximity and similarity unify a design.
b The unity of the same elements is intensified when the elements are brought into contact with each other in a continuing line.
c Pablo Picasso. *La Joie de Vivre or Antipolis.* 1946. Painting on fiber reinforced cement. 47¼ × 98½" (100 × 250 cm). Picasso Museum, Antibes, France.
d Edgar Degas. *The Tub.* 1886. Pastel, 23½ × 32⅓" (60 × 82 cm). Musée d'Orsay, Paris.
e *Flight.* March 1982. For U & LC International Typeface Corp. B. Martin Pedersen, Art Director; Jonson Pedersen Hinrichs & Shakery, Inc.

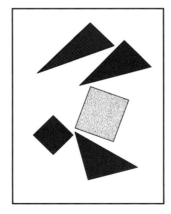

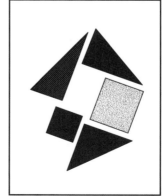

a   b

c

d

e

Ways to Achieve Unity

CONTINUATION

Continuation is the planned arrangement of various forms so that their edges are lined up—hence forms that are "continuous" from one to another within a design.

The same basic concept can be applied to the design of projects, such as pamphlets, catalogs, magazines, or books, that have many pages. Here the task of the graphic designer is not merely to achieve visual unity within a single format, but to give some sort of cohesive, unifying structure to multiple units. In effect, the device of continuation is extended and now carried through a series of related patterns. An aid often used in such serial designs is the *grid*.

The artist begins by designing a grid, a network of horizontal and vertical intersecting lines that divide the page and create a framework of areas such as **a.** Then, this same "skeleton" is used on all succeeding pages so a consistency of spacing and design results throughout all the units. To divide any format into areas or modules permits, of course, innumerable possibilities, so there is no predetermined pattern or solution. In creating the initial grid, there are often numerous technical considerations that would determine the solution. But the basic idea is easily understood.

Using the same grid (or space division) on each successive page might suggest that a sameness, and hence boring regularity, would result from repetition. This, however, is not true. A great deal of variety is possible within any framework, as the varied page layouts in **b** and **c** show.

As the computer becomes more and more important in graphic design, techniques such as the grid will become very common.

Sometimes the same grid will be used on all publications by a company so they all share a visual unity and what is called a "corporate identity." We are all familiar with examples of this. Sometimes a company, over a period of weeks or months, runs a series of advertisements that have an identical layout. The illustrations and copy change, but the basic space division stays the same. Often a single glimpse of the page identifies the advertiser in our minds because we are already so familiar with the overall format.

a A grid determines page margins and divides the format into areas used on successive layouts.
b A grid need not lead to a boring regularity in page design.
c Wide variety is possible within the basic framework.

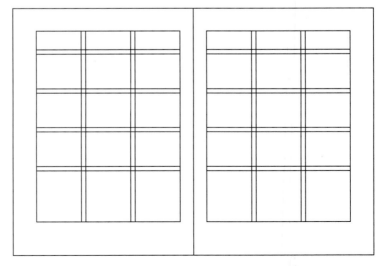

a

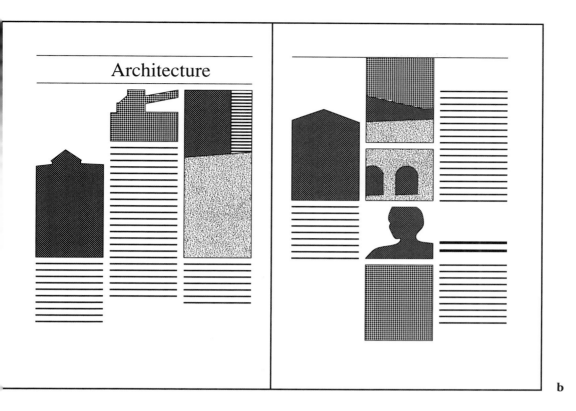

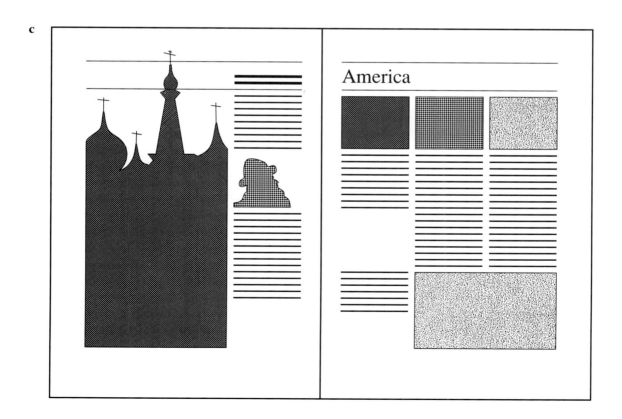

Unity with Variety

Design implies unity, a harmonious pattern or order established among the various elements. However, it is possible to make a pattern so highly unified that the result, instead of being visual satisfaction, rather quickly becomes visual boredom. The checkerboard design in **a** is an example. With its scrupulous use of proximity, constant repetition, and careful lining up of the elements, the design is an excellent example of unity—and also quite a dull thing to look at.

The designer's aim is to achieve unity, but a unity that branches out into variations that relieve boredom. *Unity with variety* is the oft-quoted artistic idea, or *theme and variations*, as the idea is aptly called in music. Shapes may repeat, but perhaps in different sizes; colors may repeat, but perhaps in different values. The easiest way to understand is to look at examples.

The Mondrian painting **(b)** in many ways resembles the checkerboard, but how much more visually interesting it is. This interest comes basically from an application of the unity-with-variety principle. The varying sizes and shapes of the rectangles, the subtle changes in the thickness of the black lines, the irregular placement of a few colored shapes, the delicate variation of horizontal and vertical emphasis—all these serve to maintain our interest far longer than does the checkerboard design.

Variety is necessary in all types of designs, not only in abstract patterns such as the Mondrian. In the seventeenth-century Dutch painting **(c)** countless rectangles can be found. These rectangles vary in size, in dark and light, and in horizontal or vertical emphasis. This overall repetition is then broken by several rounded forms that create a contrast of shape and points of accent.

The quilted tapestry **(d)** has a unity based on repetition of triangular shapes. A great deal of variety is introduced: The triangles are different sizes, and the colors and patterns of the many materials vary. Notice how the lines of stitching reinforce the triangle theme and, in effect, create countless other triangles.

a Unity without variety can result in a monotonous design.
b Piet Mondrian. *Composition with Red, Yellow, and Blue.* 1937–1942. Oil on canvas, 28⅝ × 27¼″ (73 × 69 cm). Tate Gallery, London. Reproduced by courtesy of the Trustees.
c Emmanuel de Witte. *Interior with Woman Playing the Clavecin.* 1670s. Museum Boymans-van Beuningen, Rotterdam, The Netherlands.
d Susan Hoffman. *Invention of the Spirit of J.S. Bach.* 1975. Quilted tapestry. 7′9″ × 6′10″ (2.36 × 2.08 m). Courtesy Kornblee Gallery, New York.

a

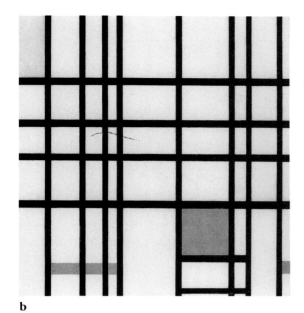

b

d

c

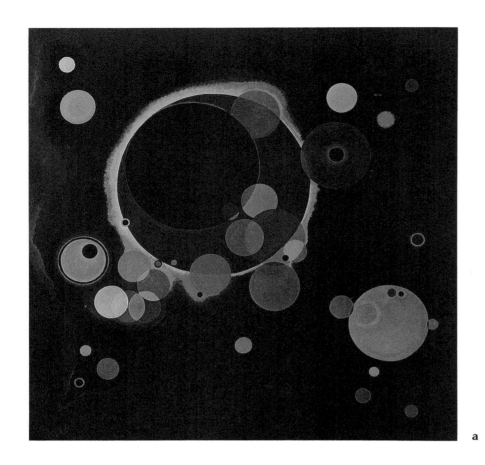

a

b

Unity with Variety

Is the principle of *unity with variety* a conscious, planned ingredient supplied by the artist or designer, or is it something that a confident designer produces automatically? There is no real answer. The only certainty is that the principle can be seen in art from every different period, culture, and geographic area.

Kandinsky's painting **(a)** is titled *Several Circles, No. 323.* The decision to create a composition unified by the repetition of circles was clearly an initial and deliberate choice by the artist. The changes in size and tone of the various circles must also have been purposeful, because these changes provide the interest of variety to the painting.

The use of unity with variety displayed by the woven fabric from Guinea **(b)** suggests a more intuitive approach. Since many such designs employ traditional motifs, the method was undoubtedly "learned," but not at an art school or from a textbook. Yet the design illustrates the principle so clearly. The basic pattern is a very simple dark-and-light checkerboard with a slight horizontal emphasis, as the areas are not square. But then horizontal variations are introduced, and not in a regular way. These linear patterns with varying weights of line and differing dark and light emphasis make a very striking pattern with very simple elements. The idea of related variations seems to provide a basic visual satisfaction that can be arrived at without theoretical discussions of aesthetics.

A conscious (or obvious) use of unity with variety does not necessarily lessen our pleasure as viewers. A very obvious use of the principle is not a drawback. Little Moreton Hall **(c)** is a visual delight. The complicated structure has been clearly unified by the lively patterns of timber and plaster that cover its exterior. Each part of the building continues the basic black-and-white design of the English Tudor *half-timbered* style. But each wing, often each floor, gives us new patterns, new motifs, and slight but definite variations. This unity didn't just happen; it was certainly carefully planned, and the result is magnificent.

---

a Wassily Kandinsky. *Several Circles, No. 323.* 1926. Oil on canvas, 4'7⅛"
(1.4 m) square. Solomon R. Guggenheim Museum, New York.
b *Men's Weave.* Woven fabric from French Guinea. 8' × 5'6"
(2.44 × 1.68 m). American Museum of Natural History, New York.
c Little Moreton Hall, Cheshire, England. Ca. 1559–1589.

c

Unity with Variety

EMPHASIS ON UNITY

In the application of any art principle, wide flexibility is possible within the general framework of the guideline. So it is with the idea of *unity with variety*. To say a design must contain both the ordered quality of unity and the lively quality of variety does not limit or inhibit the artist. The principle can encompass a wide variety of extremely different visual images.

These pages show successful examples in which the unifying element of repetition is emphasized. Variety *is* present, but admittedly in a subtle, understated way. The seventeenth-century portrait **(a)** intrigues us in the same way we are fascinated in life when we meet "identical" twins. Such perfect repetition is unexpected, so we proceed to search for the tiny differences and variety we know exists in nature and, hence, in art.

Though slightly more apparent, the variety and differences in **b** are still somewhat subtle. The aptly titled *Pies, Pies, Pies* by Wayne Thiebaud is just that: similar pieces of pie on white plates lined up in formal diagonal rows as if displayed on a cafeteria counter. The triangular wedges of pie, the elliptical plates and the cast shadows march in regular, repetitive rhythm across the canvas.

The visual unity gained by repetition is immediately apparent, in fact, almost overwhelmingly so, in **c**, an example of color-field painting. This style is sometimes referred to as Minimal Art since these artists sought to reduce art to a minimum of aesthetic considerations. To focus our attention on color relationships, subject matter is absent, and even compositional elements are purposely deemphasized. The rigidly concentric composition of squares provides no shape contrast or placement variation. Our attention must be directed to the tone and color relationships. Such paintings have sometimes been criticized as "too dull" or "too cold and sterile." Many of these comments are by people who have never read or heard of the phrase "unity with variety." Nevertheless, they are using the basic concept in their criticism. What these comments truly mean is that the design has an overwhelming unity, but the variety is so subtle as to be insufficient for the particular viewer's taste. The "correct" balance between unity and variety—between control and spontaneous freedom—varies with the individual artist, with the theme or purpose, and eventually with the viewer.

a

b

c

a

b

c

Unity with Variety

EMPHASIS ON VARIETY

Life is not always orderly and rational. Often life brings surprises, the unexpected, and experiences that seem chaotic and hectic. To express this aspect of life, many artists have purposely chosen to underplay the unifying components of their work and let the elements appear at least superficially uncontrolled and free of any formal design restraints. The examples here show works in which the element of *variety* is paramount.

The immediate impression of Richard Hamilton's collage **(a)** is one of a haphazard conglomeration of incongruous images. That, of course, is the point. The collage is as wildly eccentric as the disjointed, fragmented images we see each day (and take for granted) on our television screens and in our newspapers. The many commercial images included mock the importance of such elements in our society. Again, the theme has dictated the design.

The whimsical "toy" by Charles Eames **(b)** does have something of a unifying element in the design repetition of circles. But these circles appear in so many sizes, colors, and patterns, and in such an irregular arrangement that the effect is almost bewildering.

Also, notice that this is a solar-powered "machine," so that all these shapes would move, spin, and "whirr" in a kinetic display that is constantly changing.

Complicated, twisting linear forms dominate the Pollock painting in **c.** There is no subject matter except for the idea of dynamics and change. A feeling of unplanned, totally spontaneous movement pervades the image. In galleries or museums, when expressionist abstractions such as **c** are exhibited, one constantly overhears such criticisms as "I don't like it—too messy," "too wild and uncontrolled," and even "my 2-year-old could do *that*." What these self-styled critics are saying is that the variety in such a picture is extremely obvious, but their eyes cannot discern any sense of order or unity imposed on that variety. The scales have tipped too far in one direction for them.

Without some aspects of unity, an image becomes chaotic and quickly "unreadable." Without some elements of variety, an image is lifeless and dull and becomes uninteresting. Neither utter confusion nor utter regularity are visually desirable. Beyond this general guideline, the options of the artist are very broad.

a Richard Hamilton. *Just What Is It That Makes Today's Homes So Different, So Appealing?* 1956. Collage on paper, $10\frac{1}{8} \times 9\frac{3}{4}''$ (26 × 25 cm). Private collection.

b Charles Eames. *Solar Toy (Do Nothing Machine).* 1957. (Destroyed). Plastic and aluminum. ALCOA.

c Jackson Pollock. *Echo (Number 25, 1951).* 1951. Enamel paint on canvas, $91\frac{7}{8} \times 86''$ (233.3 × 218.4 cm). Collection, The Museum of Modern Art, New York (acquired through the Lillie P. Bliss Bequest).

3

EMPHASIS/ FOCAL POINT

Introduction

The designer's main enemy is apathy. You'd almost rather viewers would stand and revile your image than to pass it quickly with a bored "ho-hum." Your job is to catch attention and provide a pattern that stimulates the viewer by offering some visual satisfaction. Nothing will guarantee success, but one device that can help is a point of emphasis, or *focal point*. This attracts attention and encourages the viewer to look further.

In a picture or design with a theme to relate, the viewer can be shown immediately that "here is the most important character or element." *Mourning Picture* **(a)** is a haunting painting done by the American artist Edwin Romanzo Elmer soon after the death of his young daughter. The child dominates the picture and is the first thing we see. She is the largest figure and stands alone on the left side with her head carefully placed against the plain light sky. The sharp contrast of her dark and light dress with the white lamb also attracts our eye. Other elements call our attention to her, especially the light doll carriage on the lawn. The artist's chosen emphasis is unmistakable.

Even in purely abstract or nonobjective patterns, a focal point will attract the viewer's eye and give some contrast and visual emphasis. The painting by Stuart Davis **(b)** is a pattern of simple, bold forms in bright, flat colors. The more complicated curving black shape near the center provides a change and becomes the focal point.

There can be more than one focal point. Sometimes secondary points of emphasis are present that have less attention value than the focal point. These are called *accents*. A focal point and several accents can be very effective. Miro's painting **(c)** shows the effect. The focal point is obviously the pair of large, circular, black-and-white "eyes" in the lower right. This same motif is used again in several other places with less emphasis to provide contrast with the many solid black forms.

However, the designer must be careful. Several focal points of equal emphasis can turn the design into a three-ring circus in which the viewer does not know where to look first. Interest is replaced by confusion: When *everything* is emphasized, *nothing* is emphasized.

---

a Edwin Romanzo Elmer. *Mourning Picture.* 1890. Oil on canvas, 28 × 36″ (71 × 92 cm). Smith College Museum of Art (purchase).
b Stuart Davis. *Ready to Wear.* 1955. Oil on canvas, 56 × 42″ (142.9 × 106.7 cm). © 1989 The Art Institute of Chicago (gift of Mr. and Mrs. Sigmund Kunstadter). All rights reserved.
c Joan Miró. *The Beautiful Bird Revealing the Unknown to a Pair of Lovers.* 1941. Gouache and oil wash, 18 × 15″ (45.72 × 38.1 cm). Collection, The Museum of Modern Art, New York (acquired through the Lillie P. Bliss Bequest).

a

b

c

a

b

c

d

Ways to Achieve Emphasis

EMPHASIS BY CONTRAST

Very often in art the pictorial emphasis is clear, and in simple compositions (such as a portrait) the focal point is obvious. But the more complicated the pattern, the more necessary or helpful a focal point may become in organizing the design.

As a general rule, a focal point results when one element differs from the others. Whatever interrupts an overall feeling or pattern automatically attracts the eye by this difference. The possibilities are almost endless:

When most of the elements are vertical, a few horizontal forms break the pattern and become focal points.

When most of the image consists of small, busy, black-and-white patterns, a larger flat area of pure unbroken white becomes the focal point **(a)**.

In a design consisting of large smooth planes, a small, linear, detailed element is emphasized **(b)**.

When many elements are about the same size, similar but unexpectedly smaller ones become visually important **(c)**.

In a design of mainly abstract forms, the occasional recognizable image becomes a focus of attention **(d)**.

This list could go on and on; many other possibilities will occur to you. Sometimes this idea is called *emphasis by contrast*. The element that contrasts with, rather than continues, the prevailing design scheme becomes the focal point.

Color is an element often used to achieve this emphasis by contrast. A change in color or a change in brightness can immediately attract our attention.

SEE ALSO: DEVICES TO SHOW DEPTH/SIZE, PAGE 167, VALUE AS EMPHASIS, PAGE 218, AND COLOR AS EMPHASIS, PAGE 241.

a Felix Vallotton. *Laziness.* 1896. Woodcut, printed in black; block: 7⅛ × 8¹³⁄₁₆″ (18 × 21 cm). Collection, The Museum of Modern Art, New York (Larry Aldrich Fund).

b Elie Nadelman. *Man in the Open Air.* Ca. 1915. Bronze; height 4′6½″ (1.38 m); at base 11¾ × 21½″ (29.8 × 54.6 cm). Collection, The Museum of Modern Art, New York (gift of William Paley by exchange).

c Fernando Botero. *Night in Colombia.* 1980. Oil on canvas, 74 × 91″ (188 × 231.1 cm). Metropolitan Museum of Art, New York (anonymous gift, 1983).

d Ceri Richards. *Major–Minor Orange Blue.* 1970. Screenprint, 29⅞ × 21¾″ (76 × 55 cm). Courtesy Marlborough Fine Art Ltd., London.

Ways to Achieve Emphasis

EMPHASIS BY ISOLATION

A variation on the device of emphasis by contrast is the useful technique of *emphasis by isolation*. When one item is isolated or sits apart from the other elements or group of elements, it becomes a focal point. Just by its separation, an element takes on visual importance. This is contrast, of course, but it is contrast of placement, not form. In such a case, the element need not be any different from the others. The black square in **a** is like others in the design, but its placement away from them draws the eye, and it becomes the focal point.

In the still life by Cézanne **(b)** the pitcher at left repeats the color of the bowl and the cloth, and the design on it repeats the fruit forms. In short, the pitcher is part of a unified composition, but it gains visual importance because it sits away from the items grouped together at right. The pitcher is an emphasized element only through its detached position.

The theme of Gauguin's painting **(c)** is Jacob wrestling with the angel, as the subtitle tells us. Yet this main subject is quite small and spatially far away compared to other elements in the painting. However, there is no doubt as to the emphasis since these two figures are alone in the upper right of the composition. This action is isolated from the crowd of onlookers and further cut off by the large, diagonal tree trunk.

In neither of these examples is the focal point directly in the center of the composition. This could appear *too* obvious and contrived. However, it is wise to remember that a focal point placed too close to an edge will have a tendency to pull the viewer's eye right out of the picture. Notice in the Cézanne still life **(b)** how the verticals of the drapery on the left side keep the isolated pitcher from directing our gaze out of the picture. In **c** the wrestling figures are not truly on the painting's edge. With the angel's foot touching the tree trunk and his wing disappearing in the tree's foliage, the forms become a unified part of the whole composition.

---

a Isolating an element draws our attention to it.

b Paul Cézanne. *Still Life with Apples and Peaches.* Ca. 1905. Oil on canvas, 32 × 39⅝″ (81 × 100 cm). National Gallery of Art, Washington, DC (gift of Eugene and Agnes Meyer).

c Paul Gauguin. *Vision After the Sermon (Jacob Wrestling with the Angel).* 1888. Oil on canvas, 28¾ × 36⅛″ (73.03 × 91.75 cm). National Gallery of Scotland, Edinburgh.

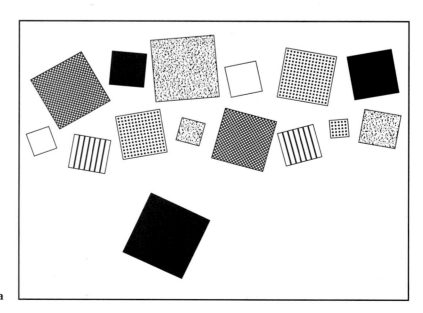

a

b

c

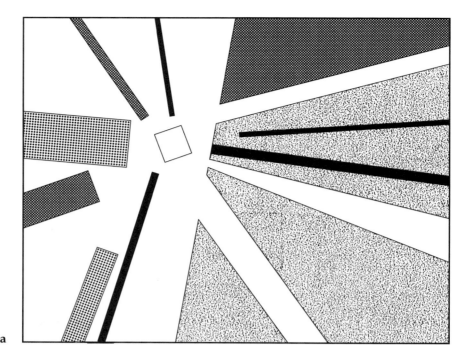

Ways to Achieve Emphasis

EMPHASIS BY PLACEMENT

The placement of elements in a design may function in another way to create emphasis. If many elements point to one item, our attention is directed there, and a focal point results. A radial design is a perfect example of this device. Just as all forms radiate from the convergent focus, so they also repeatedly lead our eyes back to this central element. As **a** illustrates, this central element may be like other forms in the design; the emphasis results from the placement, not from any difference in character, of the form itself.

Radial designs are more common in architecture or the craft areas than in two-dimensional art. The more subtle variation in painting occurs when many figures *look* (or sometimes point) in a common direction. In life when we see someone staring or pointing a certain way, we have an almost uncontrollable urge to look there. This happens in art, too. In Curry's scene of a fundamentalist baptism by immersion **(b)**, all the figures look directly at the preacher and the girl, automatically directing our eyes there as well. Even the lines of the windmill and the roofs of the barn and house direct our eyes to the focal point of these two figures.

In the photograph shown in **c,** the placement is important for emphasis. The police officer, being the only figure, is a natural focal point. Beyond this, his placement at the point where other background lines converge (especially the perspective diagonals of the brick wall) reinforces his dramatic emphasis.

The effect need not be as obvious as in these examples. However, once your focal point has been decided upon, it is wise to avoid having other major or visually important elements point or lead the eye *away* from it. Confusion of emphasis can result.

---

a Our eyes are drawn to the central element of this design by all the elements radiating from it.

b John Steuart Curry. *Baptism in Kansas.* 1928. Oil on canvas, 3'4" × 4'2" (1.02 × 1.27 m). Whitney Museum of American Art, New York (gift of Gertrude Vanderbilt Whitney).

c Bill Brandt. *Policeman in Bermonday.* N.d. Photograph.

c

Degree of Emphasis

In discussing the creation and use of a focal point, a word of warning is in order. There is no real difficulty in introducing a new contrasting element into a design. However, any emphasis must be created with some subtlety and a sense of restraint. The focal point must remain a part of the overall design, rather than become an alien element that looks totally out of place.

In the design in **a** the focal point is obvious. The large, irregular black shape is very different from the gray, rectangular shapes forming the rest of the design. It *is* a clear focal point but seems *too* strong and quite unrelated to the other elements. Rather than being a unified point of emphasis, it seems to overwhelm the rest of the design. To a lesser extent, the same criticism might apply to the painting by Bonnard **(b).** The isolated, black oval tray in the center foreground is clearly a focal point. But again, it seems almost too dominant; this sudden dark spot seems out of keeping with the subtle value and color changes in the rest of the painting.

In Juan Gris' still life **(c),** the massed group of linear circles defining the bunch of grapes is a focal point. But the values of this element are repeated in several other places. And circular forms are seen elsewhere, with the bottle top and glass bottom repeating the same small linear circle motif. The focal point established is not a completely unrelated element.

In **d** the figures in the center are clearly the focal point. While somewhat in the background, the women are rounded, irregular shapes and are surrounded and "framed" by numerous rectangles and straight lines. However, curves do appear in some other elements, noticeably the large drapery blocking part of the doorway. The light-and-dark contrast on the figures also emphasizes them when compared to the general overall dark of the foreground areas. But again the value contrast on the tiled floor and the dark pictures against the light wall keep the figures from seeming too dominant and unrelated to the rest of the painting.

A specific theme may, at times, call for a very dominant, even overwhelming, focal point. But, in general, the principle of unity and the creation of a harmonious pattern with related elements is more important than the injection of a focal point if this point would jeopardize the design's unity.

---

a The black shape seems too strong and unrelated to other elements.
b Pierre Bonnard. *Coffee.* Ca. 1914. Oil on canvas, 28¾ × 41⅞″ (73 × 106.4 cm). Tate Gallery, London. Reproduced by courtesy of the Trustees.
c Juan Gris. *Bottle, Glass and Fruit Dish.* 1921. Oil on canvas, 24 × 20″ (61 × 50 cm). Kunstmuseum Basel (Emmanuel Hoffmann-Stiftung).
d Jan Vermeer. *The Love Letter.* 1666. Oil on canvas, 17¼ × 15¼″ (44 × 39 cm). Rijksmuseum, Amsterdam.

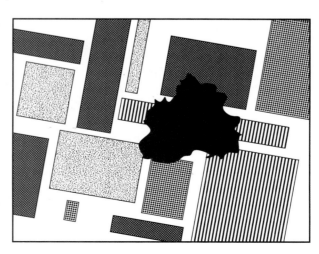

a

b

c

d

a

b

c

Absence of Focal Point

A definite focal point is not a necessity in creating a successful design. It is a tool that artists may or may not use, depending on their aims. Many paintings have an ambiguous emphasis, and different viewers will see different elements as the most important. Indeed, many artists have purposely ignored the whole idea of a focal point. Irene Rice Pereira's painting **(a)** is an example. Similar geometric forms extend over the whole painting. The artist creates an interesting feeling of depth and light that is puzzling and ambiguous. No one area stands out; the painting has no real starting point or visual climax.

Sometimes the artist's theme might suggest the absence of a focal point. In Andy Warhol's painting **(b)** there are a hundred repetitions of precisely the same image with no change, no contrast, and no point of emphasis. But the repetitive, unrelieved quality is the basic point and dictated the design. The painting contains a serious comment on our taken-for-granted daily lives. The design reflects life today, where we are bombarded with insistent and strident repetition of the same commercial images over and over.

Some art forms by their very nature rule out the use of a focal point. Woven and printed fabrics generally have no focal point but consist of an unstressed repetition of a motif over the whole surface. A focal point on draperies, bedspreads, or upholstery might be distracting. In clothing, the focal point is provided by the design of the garment.

Since a focal point is such a common artistic device, sometimes attention can be gotten by simply *not* using one. There is no dominant element in the poster in **c.** Instead, we are intrigued by the pattern of widely different items, all with equal emphasis. The designer has achieved his goal: Our eye is attracted by the unusual overall emphasis of the layout, and we spend time studying the image.

SEE ALSO: CRYSTALLOGRAPHIC BALANCE, PAGE 77.

a Irene Rice Pereira. *Green Depth.* 1944. Oil on canvas, 31 × 42″ (79 × 107 cm). Metropolitan Museum of Art, New York (George A. Hearn Fund, 1944).

b Andy Warhol. *100 Cans.* 1962. Oil on canvas. 6′ × 4′4″ (1.83 × 1.32 m). Albright-Knox Art Gallery, Buffalo, New York (gift of Seymour H. Knox, 1963).

c *Seasons Greetings from WGBH Design.* Poster. 1985. 37 × 32″ (94 × 81.3 cm). Chris Pullman, Art Director; Gaye Korbet and Chris Pullman, Designers.

CHAPTER

BALANCE

Introduction

Example **a** is a cropped detail showing only a part of a portrait by Thomas Eakins. The entire painting is shown in **b.** Why do we find **b** a more satisfactory image than **a?** Partially, of course, because we like to see more of the subject; cutting through the woman's face seems curious. But the main reason for our preference concerns the principle of *balance.* Without showing the chair and the position of the woman within the surrounding space **(a),** all the visual weight rests on the left side. There is nothing on the right side to compensate and provide any sort of equilibrium. The detail is off balance. The total painting shows a much more equal distribution of weight.

A sense of balance is innate; as children we develop a sense of balance in our bodies and observe balance in the world around us. Lack of balance, or *imbalance,* disturbs us. We carefully avoid dangerously leaning trees, rocks, furniture, and ladders. But even where no physical danger is present, as in a design or painting, we still feel more comfortable with a balanced pattern **(c).**

In assessing pictorial balance, we always assume a center vertical axis and usually expect to see some kind of equal weight (visual weight) distribution on either side. This axis functions as the fulcrum on a scale or seesaw, and the two sides should achieve a sense of equilibrium. When this equilibrium is not present, as in **d,** a certain vague uneasiness or dissatisfaction results. We feel a need to rearrange the elements, in the same way that we automatically straighten a tilted picture on the wall.

---

a Thomas Eakins. *Miss Van Buren,* detail.
b Thomas Eakins. *Miss Van Buren.* Ca. 1886–1890. Oil on canvas, 45 × 32″ (114.3 × 81.2 cm). Phillips Collection, Washington, DC.
c Paolo Veronese. *Christ in the House of Levi.* 1573. Oil on canvas, 18′2″ × 42′ (5.54 × 12.8 m). Accademia, Venice.
d An unbalanced design leaves the viewer with a vague uneasiness.

a   b

c

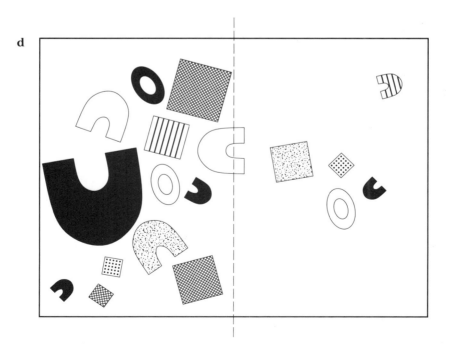

d

a

c

b

Introduction

Balance—some equal distribution of visual weight—is a universal aim of composition. The vast majority of pictures we see have been consciously balanced by the artist. However, this does not mean there is no place in art for purposeful imbalance. An artist may, because of a particular theme or topic, expressly desire that a picture raise uneasy, disquieting responses in the viewer. In this instance, imbalance can be a useful tool. Even without such a motive, an occasional almost imbalanced image, such as that in the Daumier drawing **(a)**, intrigues us and attracts our attention for exactly this unexpected quality.

In speaking of pictorial balance, we are almost always referring to horizontal balance, the right and left sides of the image. Artists consider vertical balance as well, with a horizontal axis dividing top and bot-tom. Again a certain general equilibrium is usually desirable. However, because of our sense of gravity, we are accustomed to seeing more weight toward the bottom, with a resulting stability and calm **(b).** The farther up in the format the main distribution of weight or visual interest occurs, the more unstable and dynamic the image becomes.

The effect can be seen in Kandinsky's pen and ink drawing **(c).** The inverted triangular shapes are piled up in a precarious manner as weight increases higher on the format. In Paul Klee's whimsical *Tight-rope Walker* **(d),** the instability of the image expresses the theme perfectly. The linear patterns build up verti-cally until we reach the teetering figure near the top. The artist can manipulate the vertical balance freely to fit a particular theme or purpose.

a Honoré Daumier. *Connoisseurs.* Water, charcoal, pen and ink, 10¾ × 7⅝″ (27.3 × 19.4 cm). The Cleveland Museum of Art (Dudley P. Allen Fund).

b Canaletto. *The Basin of St. Mark's, Venice.* 1735–1741. Oil on canvas, 4 × 6′ (1.21 × 1.83 m). National Gallery, London. Reproduced by courtesy of the Trustees.

c Wassily Kandinsky. *Untitled Drawing.* 1932. Pen and ink on paper, 13¾ × 9″ (35 × 22.9 cm). Collection, The Josef Albers Foundation, New Haven, CT.

d Paul Klee. *Tightrope Walker,* plate 4 from the portfolio *Mappe der Gegenwart.* 1923. Color lithograph, 17⅛ × 10⅝″ (44 × 26 cm). Collection, The Museum of Modern Art, New York (given anonymously).

d

Symmetrical Balance

The simplest type of balance, both to create and to recognize, is called *symmetrical* balance. In symmetrical balance, like shapes are repeated in the same positions on either side of a central vertical axis **(a).** One side, in effect, becomes the mirror image of the other side. Symmetrical balance has a seemingly basic appeal for us. Children and beginning art students will almost instinctively create patterns with symmetrical balance. Psychologists ascribe this to our awareness of the fact that our bodies are basically symmetrical, so that we intuitively extend the principle to our first artistic efforts.

Conscious symmetrical repetition, while clearly creating perfect balance, can be undeniably static, so that the term *formal* balance is used to describe the same idea. There is nothing wrong with quiet formality. In fact, this characteristic is often desired in some art, notably in architecture. Countless examples of architecture with symmetrical balance can be found throughout the world dating from most periods of art history. The continuous popularity of symmetrical design is not hard to understand. The formal quality in symmetry imparts an immediate feeling of permanence, strength, and stability. Such qualities are important in public buildings to suggest the dignity and power of a government. So, statehouses, city halls, palaces, courthouses, and other government monuments often exploit the properties of symmetrical balance.

The art museum in Portland, Maine **(b)** has a rigidly repetitive pattern, and the result is a sedate, calm, and dignified facade. Such an effect is often termed *classical,* alluding to the many ancient Greek and Roman buildings in which symmetrical design imparted the same feeling of clarity and rational order.

Symmetrical balance does not, by itself, preordain any specific visual result. Examples **b** and **c** are both symmetrical facades, but here the similarity ends. The stark simplicity of the museum **(b)** with the orderly progression of a few repeated shapes and a calm, regular rhythm of dark and light is certainly not present in the Spanish cathedral **(c).** The latter is a busy, excitingly ornate building with only the symmetrical organization molding the masses of niches, balustrades, columns, and statuary into a unified and coherent visual pattern.

---

a In symmetrical balance, one side of a design mirrors the other.
b Henry N. Cobb/I.M. Pei and Partners. Portland Museum of Art, Portland, ME. 1983.
c José Peña and Fernando de Casas. Cathedral. Santiago de Compostela, Spain. 1667–1750.

a

b

c

a

b

Symmetrical Balance

Symmetrical balance is rarer in painting than in architecture. In fact, relatively few paintings would fit a strict definition of symmetry.

Trumbull's painting **(a)** would commonly be termed a symmetrical composition. However the groups of soldiers on either side of the centered generals are obviously not identical. Rarely do paintings repeat *exactly* the same elements on both sides. Sometimes the term *near symmetry* is used to describe this effect: elements or figures on opposing sides may vary, but being so nearly alike do not change the initial overall impression of symmetrical balance.

Sometimes the subject matter makes symmetrical balance an appropriate compositional device. A dignified, solemn subject as the Madonna enthroned **(b)** clearly calls for the stable, calm qualities symmetrical balance can impart. In this example, while the architectural setting is completely symmetrical, the saints flanking the Madonna are again similar but not identical.

Both paintings **a** and **b** show one distinct advantage to symmetrical compositions: the immediate creation and emphasis of a focal point. With the two sides being so much alike, there is an obvious visual importance to whatever element is placed on the center axis.

Quiet formality is certainly not a characteristic of **c.** A painting based on the innumerable rock posters from the psychedelic, drug-oriented culture of the 1960s is perhaps the last place we would expect to find symmetrical balance. But it illustrates another use of symmetry. If the artist's design involves a great number of figures or elements, then symmetrical balance (which in other cases appears a rather contrived device) can organize a possible confusion into a readable pattern. In this painting **(c)** only the symmetrical repetition keeps a fantastically complicated design of "jumpy" shapes organized and at least somewhat coherent. Thus, the simplicity of symmetrical balance can be an asset if the design elements are busy and complex.

---

a John Trumbull. *The Surrender of Lord Cornwallis.* 1787–1794. Oil on canvas, 20⅞ × 30⅝" (53 × 78 cm). Copyright Yale University Art Gallery, New Haven, CT.

b Domenico Veneziano. *The St. Lucy Altarpiece.* Ca. 1445. Tempera on wood panel, approx. 6'7½" × 7' (2.02 × 2.13 m). Galleria degli Uffizi, Florence.

c Karl Wirsum. *Screamin' Jay Hawkins.* 1968. Acrylic on canvas, 47½ × 37" (122 × 91 cm). © 1989 Art Institute of Chicago (Mr. and Mrs. Frank G. Logan A.I.C. Prize Fund and Logan Fund Income). All rights reserved.

c

Asymmetrical Balance

INTRODUCTION

The second type of balance is called *asymmetrical* balance. In this case, balance is achieved with *dissimilar* objects that have equal visual weight or equal eye attraction. Remember the children's riddle: "Which weighs more, a pound of feathers or a pound of lead?" Of course, they both weigh a pound, but the amount and mass of each vary radically. This, then, is the essence of asymmetrical balance.

In Mary Cassatt's painting **(a),** the figures are not centered on the canvas. They are completely on the left side of the center axis. But the composition is not off balance. The right side shows a close view of the shiny, reflective silver tea set and tray. There is also the fireplace and over-the-mantel elements that provide more complicated forms than the repetitive striped wallpaper behind the figures. The two sides of the picture are thus very different, with quite dissimilar elements, yet a sense of balance is maintained as each side provides equal visual attraction.

The painting shows one advantage of asymmetrical balance. It is casual, not contrived or posed in feeling. The alternate title *informal* balance is often used, and the term is appropriate. This painting *is* informal. This feeling stems not solely from the woman in the momentary act of drinking her tea, but from the whole composition that, at first glance, appears completely natural and, indeed, unplanned. A symmetrical arrangement of the same elements was certainly possible, but the effect would be totally different.

Symmetry can appear artificial, as our visual experiences in life are rarely symmetrically arranged. Some buildings and interiors are so designed, but even here unless we stand quietly at dead center, our views are always asymmetrical. Asymmetry appears casual and less planned, although obviously this characteristic is misleading. Asymmetrical balance is actually more intricate and complicated to use than symmetrical balance. Merely repeating similar elements in a mirror image on either side of the center is not a difficult design task. But attempting to balance *dis*similar items involves more complex considerations and more subtle factors.

The contrast possible in asymmetrical balance can be seen in **b.** This Tokyo building is a combination office and living space. On a small site, a great contrast of bold elements in asymmetrical balance creates a dynamic visual pattern. On the left is a large, plain wall of horizontal tiles, which shields the spaces behind it. On the right, an unexpected dark wedge juts out over the geometric lower office entrance. A gold, accordion-pleated element connects the two areas. Balance is achieved with very dissimilar elements.

The sculpture by Richard Artschwager **(c)** shows the extreme differences that asymmetrical balance can accommodate. The several black (almost floating) geometric forms on the right are visually balanced by the rectangular block base painted in a bold, waving, striped pattern on the left.

---

a Mary Stevenson Cassatt. *A Cup of Tea.* Ca. 1880. Oil on canvas, 25½ × 36½" (65 × 93 cm). Courtesy Museum of Fine Arts, Boston (M. Theresa B. Hopkins Fund).

b Atsushi Kitagawara/ILCD, Inc. 395 Minami-Aoyama, Tokyo.

c Richard Artschwager. *Up and Across.* 1984–85. Polychrome on wood, 5'1" × 12' × 2'11" (1.55 × 3.66 × .9 m). Private collection. Courtesy Leo Castelli Gallery.

a

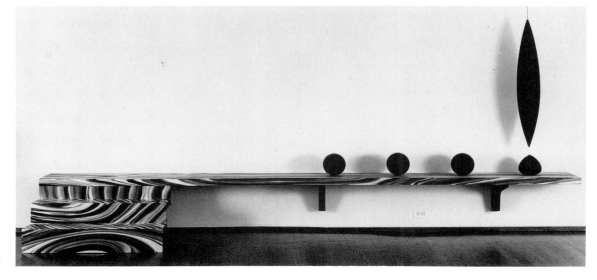

b

c

Asymmetrical Balance

BALANCE BY VALUE AND COLOR

Asymmetrical balance is based on equal eye attraction—dissimilar objects are equally interesting to the eye. One element that attracts our attention is *value* difference, a contrast of light and dark. Example **a** illustrates that black against white gives a stronger contrast than gray against white; therefore, a smaller amount of black is needed to visually balance a larger amount of gray.

This idea is illustrated in the photograph of the cathedral at York **(b)**. The left side of the composition shows many details of the angled wall of the church nave. However, the receding arches, piers, columns, and so on, are shown in subtle gradations of gray, all very close and related in value. In contrast, on the right side is the large black silhouette of a foreground column and the small window area of bright white. These two sharp visual accents of white and black are on the right and balance the many, essentially gray, elements on the left.

In **c** the figures of the mother and the child in his chair dominate the left side of the composition. The right side is balanced by the brilliant white areas of the glass lampshade and the table top which highly contrast with the overall darkness of the rest of the drawing.

An everyday carton of eggs makes a sophisticated composition due to the asymmetrical balance **(d)**. The carton is shifted to the right in this pencil drawing. The carton's light flap against the dark background and the empty dark holes provide value accents to balance the offset subject matter, the eggs on the right providing lesser contrast.

Like value contrast, color itself can be a balancing element. Studies have proven that our eyes are attracted to color. Given a choice, we will always look at a colored image rather than at one in black and white. A small area of bright color can balance a much larger area of a duller, more neutral color. Our eyes, drawn by the color, see the smaller element to be as interesting and as "heavy" visually as the larger element.

Balance by value or color is a valuable tool allowing a great difference of shapes on either side of the center axis and still achieving equal eye attraction.

SEE ALSO: COLOR AND BALANCE, PAGE 243

a A darker, smaller element is visually equal to a lighter, larger one.

b Frederic H. Evans. *York Minster, Into the South Transept.* Ca. 1900. Platinum print mounted on a sheet of brown paper upon a natural Japanese paper upon a larger sheet of gray paper. 8¼ × 4¾" (20.9 × 12.1 cm). Metropolitan Museum of Art, New York (Alfred Stieglitz Collection).

c Käthe Kollwitz. *Mother and Child by Lamplight at the Table (Self Portrait with Son, Hans?)* 1894. Pen and ink with brush and wash, 8 × 10⅝" (21 × 27 cm). Courtesy Deutsche Fotothek Dresden.

d Mark Adams. *Box of Eggs.* 1968. Pencil, 13¼ × 16¼" (34 × 41 cm). Collection Mrs. Daniel Mendelowitz.

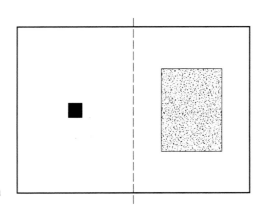

a

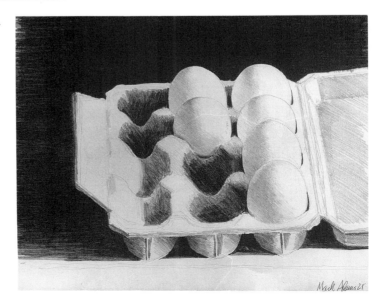

Asymmetrical Balance

BALANCE BY SHAPE AND TEXTURE

The diagram in **a** illustrates balance by shape. Here the two elements are exactly the same color, exactly the same value and texture. The only difference is their shape. The smaller form attracts the eye because of its more complicated contours. Though small, it is as interesting as the much larger, but duller, rectangle.

This type of balance appears in Mary Cassatt's painting **(b).** On the right side is the lady opera-goer, a large but fairly simple shape, mostly just a black silhouette. The left side is composed of small, more complicated shapes suggesting the audience in the more distant theater boxes. Together, they achieve balance.

The balance of the elements in the Japanese woodcut **(c)** shows the same idea. The large simple, triangular mass of the mountain is positioned to the right. The left side is balanced by the smaller, busy shapes of the clouds and the mass of small dark triangles that suggests a forest of trees. Even the symbols of the artist's signature marks provide balance on the left.

Any visual (or photographic) texture with a variegated dark and light pattern holds more interest for the eye than does a smooth, unrelieved surface. The drawing in **d** presents this idea: The smaller, rough-textured area balances the larger, basically untextured area (smoothness is, in a sense, a "texture").

The left side of the photograph in **e** attracts our attention with the architectural details and pipes in sharp light with dark shadows. The right side has fewer elements, but the brick texture and especially the repetitive horizontal design of light and dark texture on the corrugated iron door with its peeling paint is the balancing element.

Printed text consisting of letters and words in effect creates a visual texture. This is information in symbols that we can read, but the *visual* effect is nothing more than a gray-patterned shape. Depending on the typeface and the layout, this gray area varies in darkness, density, and character, but it is visually textured. Very often in advertisements or editorial page layouts an area of "textured" printed matter will balance a pictorial element.

---

a A small, complicated shape is balanced by a larger, more stable shape.

b Mary Stevenson Cassatt. *At the Opera.* 1880. Oil on canvas, 31½ × 25½" (80 × 65 cm). Courtesy Museum of Fine Arts, Boston (Charles Henry Hayden Fund).

c Katsushika Hokusai. *Fuji in Clear Weather* from *Thirty-Six Views of Fuji.* Ca. 1820–1830. Color woodcut, 10 × 15" (25 × 28 cm). Metropolitan Museum of Art, New York (bequest of Henry L. Phillips, 1939).

d A small textured shape can balance a larger untextured one.

e Mark Feldstein. *Untitled.* Photograph.

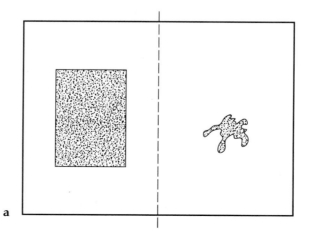

a

b

c

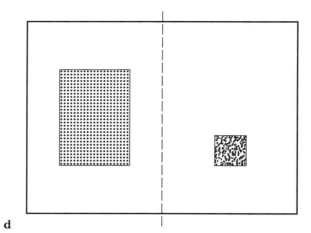

d

e

Asymmetrical Balance

BALANCE BY POSITION AND EYE DIRECTION

The two seesaw diagrams in **a** illustrate the idea of balance by position. A well-known principle in physics is that two items of unequal weight can be brought to equilibrium by moving the heavier inward toward the fulcrum. In design this means that a large item placed closer to the center can be balanced by a smaller item placed out toward the edge.

Balance by position often lends an unusual, unexpected quality to the composition. The effect not only appears casual and unplanned but also can make the composition seem, at first glance, to be in imbalance. This casual impression can be seen in a painting by Gainsborough **(b)** that features an obvious emphasis on the left, where the two figures are posed before a large tree. The three detailed trees and the wheat sheaves are smaller elements, but their placement at far right, running off the edge of the picture, provides a very subtle balance.

The same principle is used in **c,** a still life of simplified, abstracted forms. Larger objects are grouped on the left. The neck of the guitar creates a strong horizontal line that leads our eyes to the right.

On the right edge of the painting, the smaller, isolated bottle balances the heavier objects on the other side. It is often interesting to mentally move elements in paintings and see how the balance is affected.

One further element in achieving asymmetrical balance should be noted. In **d** the many heavier elements on the right all direct our attention automatically to the left, thus building up the smallest of elements into a balancing importance. Asymmetrical balance is based on equal eye attraction, and here the large elements themselves make the small element the focal point.

The technique is used in the Art Deco railway poster **(e).** The large dark locomotive is positioned on the left, but the accentuated perspective lines of the receding train and platform make a sharp arrow that directs attention to the right. Actually, only a few lines of the distant station and the tiny engineer's figure are on the right side but the eye direction creates the optical balance.

While not usually the *only* technique of balance employed, the useful device of eye direction is a common practice among artists. Eye direction is carefully plotted by the artist, not only for balance but also for general compositional unity.

---

a A large shape placed near the middle of a design can be balanced by a smaller shape placed toward the outer edge.

b Thomas Gainsborough. *Mr. and Mrs. Robert Andrews.* Ca. 1748–1750. Oil on canvas, 27 × 47" (69 × 119 cm). National Gallery, London. Reproduced by courtesy of the Trustees.

c Le Corbusier. *Still Life.* 1920. Oil on canvas, 31⅞ × 39¼" (81 × 100 cm). Collection, The Museum of Modern Art, New York (Van Gogh Purchase Fund).

d A single small element can be as important as many larger ones if it is made the focal point of the design.

e Pierre Fix-Masseau. *Exactitude.* Gouache, after a poster of 1929. 39⅜ × 24½" (100 × 62 cm). Metropolitan Museum of Art, New York (gift of the Publisher's Office, 1983).

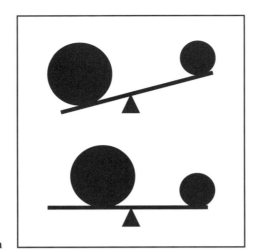

a

b

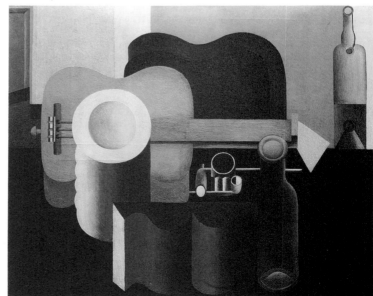

c

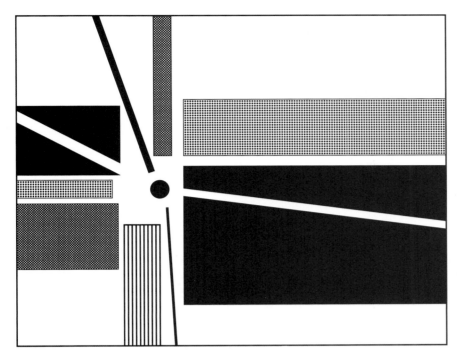

d

e

Asymmetrical Balance

ANALYSIS SUMMARY

In looking at paintings, you will realize that isolating one technique of asymmetrical balance as we have done is a bit misleading, since the vast majority of works employ several of the methods simultaneously. For the sake of clarity these methods are discussed separately, but the principles often overlap and are frequently used together. Let us look at just a few examples that make use of several of the factors involved in asymmetrical balance.

The painting by Whistler (a) would appear, at first glance, to be unbalanced, as the large, dominant figure is on the left side of the composition. The painting seems casual, almost unplanned. But this informal feeling is deceiving; a visual balance has been carefully planned. Of course, the visual emphasis is initially on the figure at the left, but many devices help to balance the right side. First of all, to balance the large (but rather simple) shape of the girl, many small, more complicated shapes appear on the right: the items on the mantel and the flower blossoms entering the format from the lower right. These items are at the right edge of the canvas. Value contrast is used. The girl is a light area with only fairly subtle value changes defining the dress. On the right there are more emphasized value changes, especially the dark fireplace contrasting with the light molding. Eye direction is an obvious factor. The girl looks to the right and the extended arm carries our eye that way. Even the decorative fan in her right hand leads our eye to the right and the flowers. And, while not apparent here, color is involved—the small bowl directly behind the girl's wrist is red, a bright color note in a fairly neutral painting.

Painting **b,** by the American artist Richard Diebenkorn, while in a very different style, has the same informal feeling as **a.** Again, there is a great deal of weight on the left side, where both figures are placed, as well as the background windows. In addition, the woman's detailed striped skirt attracts attention in a work where most of the areas are large, flat, abstracted forms. The obvious balancing element is the diagonal stripe on the floor, which forms an "arrow" directing our eye to the right. This strong light shape against the dark floor immediately attracts our attention. Dark and light contrast also emphasizes the right doorway. Repeating the vertical shape of the figures in a painting filled with horizontal emphasis, the doorway also sits at the very edge of the canvas, thus balancing by position. Finally, through the open door numerous small shapes suggesting the distant landscape can be seen. These small forms provide a visual interest lacking in the totally blank white windows on the left. The painting, therefore, uses several devices to establish a subtle sense of balance, while retaining the immediate effect of spontaneous informality.

Notice how shape, value, position, and eye direction are all involved in balancing the Japanese print in **c.**

a

b

c

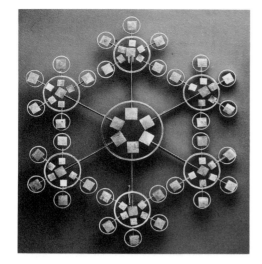

a

b

c

Radial Balance

A third variety of balance is called *radial* balance. Here all the elements radiate or circle out from a common central point. The sun with its emanating rays is a familiar symbol that expresses the basic idea. Radial balance is not entirely distinct from symmetrical or asymmetrical balance. It is merely a refinement of one or the other, depending on whether the focus occurs in the middle or off center.

Circular forms abound in craft areas such as ceramics, where the round shapes of dishes and bowls often make radial balance a natural choice in decorating such objects. Radial balance also appears in jewelry design. The brooch in **a** is reminiscent of the radial patterns found in snowflakes. Notice how each of the small outer elements makes a radial design in itself. Radial balance has been used frequently in architecture. The round form of domed buildings such as the Roman Pantheon or our nation's Capitol will almost automatically give a radial feeling to the interior.

The major compositional advantage in radial balance is the immediate and obvious creation of a focal point. Perhaps this is also the reason that such balance seldom occurs in painting. It might seem a little too contrived and unnatural, a little too obvious to be entirely satisfactory. There can be no doubt that when radial balance *is* used in painting, it is employed in a rather understated manner. Utrillo's Parisian street scene **(b)** has a quite clear radial feeling. The one-point perspective of the receding curbs and rooflines directs the eye to the white cathedral in the distance.

Radial balance may be rare in formal narrative painting, but this should not deter you from experimenting with it. It can be a useful tool in organization, and some extremely effective designs may result.

The dramatic painting by Judy Chicago **(c)** is clearly a radial pattern. The abstracted forms have a feeling of flower shapes and also (as intended) are suggestive of the theme of feminine sexuality.

a Bent Exner. Brooch in white gold and tugtupite, created for H.R.H. Queen Ingrid of Denmark. 1970. Denmark.

b Maurice Utrillo. *Church of Le Sacré Coeur, Montmartre et rue Saint-Rustique.* N.d. Oil on canvas, 19⅝ × 24" (50 × 61 cm). Courtesy, Museum of Fine Arts, Boston (bequest of John T. Spaulding).

c Judy Chicago. *The Rejection Quintet: Female Rejection Drawing.* 1974. Prismacolor and graphite on ragboard, 39⅝ × 29⅝" (100.6 × 75.2 cm). San Francisco Museum of Modern Art.

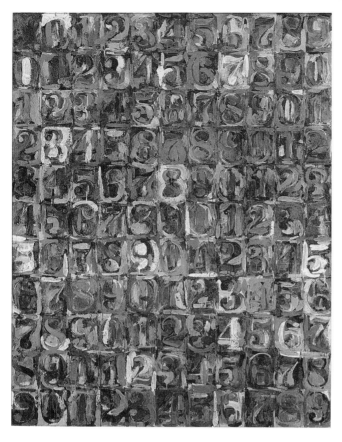

Crystallographic Balance

ALLOVER PATTERN

One more specific type of visual effect is often designated as a fourth variety of balance. The examples here illustrate the idea. These works all exhibit an equal emphasis over the whole format—the same weight or eye attraction literally everywhere. This is officially called *crystallographic balance*. Since few people can remember this term, and even fewer can spell it, the more common name is *allover pattern*. This is, of course, a rather special refinement of symmetrical balance. The constant repetition of the same quality everywhere on the surface, however, *is* truly a different impression from our usual concept of symmetrical balance.

In Jasper Johns' painting **(a),** there is uniform emphasis throughout. The many numbers appear in the same size, with each defined in the same loose, fluid brushstroke and paint texture. Value changes are interesting but are also quite evenly distributed. There is no beginning, no end, and no focal point—unless, indeed the whole picture is the focal point.

Fabric patterns, with their purposeful lack of any focal point, are usually distinguished by a constant repetition of the same motif. The nineteenth-century quilt in **b** does not repeat the same pattern over and over. Indeed, there is a wonderful variety of rich decorative patterns. But while each intricate sewn square section is different, there is equal emphasis and weight everywhere.

Both **a** and **b** are quite active visual patterns with a great complexity of forms. This is not, of course, always true of crystallographic designs. The painting by Larry Poons **(c)** is very simple. The whole composition consists of merely the repetition of dots in various colors and values. The dots are randomly placed, but are distributed quite evenly throughout the design. The dots are all the same, and no one dot (or group) stands out to provide a point of emphasis.

a Jasper Johns. *Numbers in Color.* 1959. Encaustic and newspaper on canvas, 5'6½" × 4'1⅛" (1.69 × 1.26 m). Albright-Knox Art Gallery, Buffalo, NY (gift of Seymour H. Knox, 1959).

b Quilt. Ca. 1885. America Hurrah Antiques, New York.

c Larry Poons. *Away Out on the Mountain.* 1965. Acrylic on canvas, 6 × 12' (1.83 × 3.66 m). Allen Memorial Art Museum, Oberlin College, OH (Ruth C. Roush Fund for Contemporary Art).

c
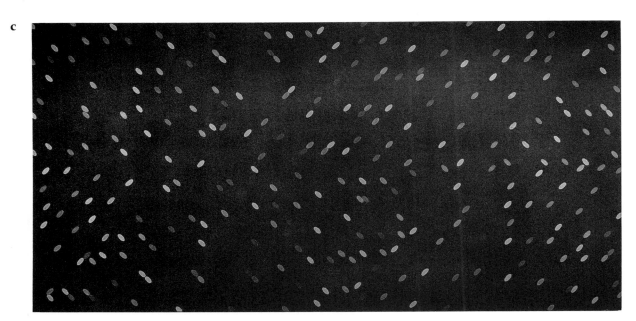

C H A P T E R

SCALE/PRO-PORTION

Introduction

Scale and *proportion* are related terms in that both refer basically to size. Scale is essentially another word for size; "large scale" is a way of saying big, and "small scale" means small. "Big" and "small," however, are relative. What is big? Big is meaningless unless we have some standard of reference. A *big* dog means nothing if we do not know the size of most dogs. This is what separates the two terms. *Proportion* refers to *relative* size, size measured against other elements or against some mental norm or standard. Look at the design in **a.** Here the large black circle would certainly be called large scale. It is a large element and occupies much space, given the overall dimensions of the design. It could also be described as out of *proportion.* Compared to the other, tinier elements it is *too* large and overwhelms the rest of the pattern, demanding all our visual attention. When the life-drawing instructor criticizes the "proportions" of a student's drawing, it means the relative sizes of the various body parts are incorrect.

We often think of the word *proportion* in connection with mathematical systems of numerical ratios. It is true that historically many such systems have been developed. Artists attempted to define the most pleasing size relationships in items as diverse as the width and length of sides of a rectangle to parts of the human body.

Scale and proportion are closely tied to emphasis and focal point. Large scale and especially large scale in proportion to other elements make for an obvious visual emphasis. In **b** the eye goes naturally first to the large-scale figure in the center. The artist, Honoré Sharrer, has created a focal point that dominates the other, smaller figures in the windows of the building in the background.

In past centuries, visual scale was often related to thematic importance. The size of figures was based on their symbolic importance in the subject being presented. In the tenth-century illumination **(c),** the emperor on his throne has been drawn unnaturally large compared to the other figures. The artist thus immediately established not only an obvious focal point but indicated the relative conceptual status of the ruler and his subjects. This use of scale is called *hieratic scaling.*

SEE ALSO: DEVICES TO SHOW DEPTH/SIZE, PAGES 167–169.

a The large circle, out of proportion to the other elements, overwhelms them.

b Honoré Sharrer. *The Industrial Scene.* Center panel of *Tribute to the American Working People.* 1945–1950. Oil on canvas, 25 × 31" (63 × 79 cm). Whereabouts unknown.

c Emperor Otto II from the *Registrum Gregorii.* Trier, Ca. 985. Manuscript illumination, 10⅝ × 7⅞" (27 × 20 cm). Musée Condé, Chantilly.

a

b

c

a

b

c

Scale of Art

There are two ways to think of artistic scale. One is to consider the scale of the work itself—its size in relation to other art, in relation to its surroundings, or in relation to human size. Unhappily, the one thing book illustrations cannot do is show art in its original size or scale. Unusual or unexpected scale is arresting and attention getting. Sheer size *does* impress us.

When we are confronted by frescoes such as the Sistine Chapel ceiling, our first reaction is simply awe at the enormous scope of the work. Later, we study and admire details, but first we are overwhelmed by the sheer magnitude. The reverse effect is illustrated in **a.** It comes as a shock to stand before this actual painting, for it is tiny—5 inches by 5 ¾ inches—barely larger than its reproduction here. The exquisite detail, the delicate precision of the drawing, and the color subtleties all impress us. Our first thought has to be of the fantastic difficulty of achieving such effects in so tiny a format.

If large or small size springs naturally from the function, theme, or purpose of a work, an unusual scale is justified. We are acquainted with many such cases. The gigantic pyramids made a political statement of the Pharaoh's eternal power. The elegant miniatures of the religious book of hours **(b)** served as book illustrations for the private devotionals of medieval nobility. The Japanese sculpture in **c** is only 2 inches tall—smaller than you see it in the picture. This tiny piece of ivory carving had a utilitarian purpose. Called a *netsuke*, the piece was a small toggle (or clip) that secured pouches and other items hung from the Japanese *obi* or waist sash. In this intricately detailed example, a scholar rides through waves on a horned carp with tiny black coral-inlaid eyes.

The scale of **d** is the opposite approach. The scale of Kent Twitchell's enormous 40-feet-high wall painting dwarfs even today's large billboards. The cars photographed in the foreground give a feeling of the work's tremendous size. The naturalistic images blown up to such monumental scale cannot be ignored, and they alter the urban environment.

---

a Follower of Jan van Eyck. *St. Francis Receiving the Stigmata.* Early 15th century. Oil on panel, 5 × 5¾" (13 × 15 cm). Galleria Sabauda, Turin.

b Limbourg Brothers. *Multiplication of the Loaves and Fishes,* from the Book of Hours *(Les Très Riches Heures)* of the Duke of Berry. 1416. Manuscript illumination, 6¼ × 4⅜" (16 × 11 cm). Musée Condé, Chantilly.

c Japanese Netsuke (Detail). 18th century. Ivory, with lacquer inro and silver ojime. Height 2" (5.1 cm). Metropolitan Museum of Art, New York (bequest of Mrs. H.O. Havemeyer, 1929, The H.O. Havemeyer Collection).

d Kent Twitchell. *The Holy Trinity with the Virgin.* 1977–1978. Acrylic wall painting, 40 × 56' (12.2 × 17.1 m). Otis/Parsons Art Institute, Los Angeles.

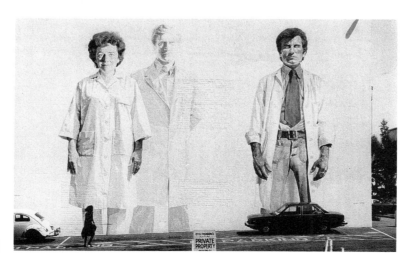

d

Scale of Art

The Bulgarian-American artist Christo has conceived and constructed unique landscape projects that are truly gigantic in scale. His *Valley Curtain* hung an orange curtain between two mountains in Colorado. The *Running Fence* ran over 24 $\frac{1}{2}$ miles of rolling hills in suburban and rural California. The sheer scale of such works was impressive. Another project has involved islands in Biscayne Bay, Florida **(a).** Eleven islands were surrounded by wide pink fabric panels (or "skirts" as some observers dubbed them). Again, the scope of the project was tremendous, involving 6 $\frac{1}{2}$ million square feet of floating fabric. Whether viewed from the shore, from a boat, or from the air, observers saw a familiar landscape environment in a suddenly new and altered context. Public controversy often accompanies these projects, although one could argue a traditional link to the past in the huge earthworks constructed in many regions of the world by ancient peoples.

Probably no motif from contemporary art has been reproduced so many times for so many different purposes as Robert Indiana's *Love* **(b).** It has been the decorative theme of T-shirts, coffee mugs, matchbook covers, wall posters, bracelet charms, postage stamps, cocktail napkins, and myriad other items. In each medium, it has changed scale, but each time it remained graphically appealing to a large audience.

Unusual scale in a work of art should have a thematic or functional justification. The painting in **c** measures 5 $\frac{1}{2}$ feet by 6 feet. This is quite large for a painting, and with its few elements and very simple spatial pattern, the large size might seem misguided. However, *Actual Size* is described by the artist, Edward Ruscha, as a "commercial landscape." Thus, the painting is a satire that is meant to mock the large scale and often inane content of the huge, strident billboards that demand our attention each day. The work's scale is an intrinsic part of the theme.

Here again the idea of proportion can be relevant. Works of art are often selected (or created) for specific locations, and their size in proportion to the setting is a prime consideration. A small religious painting appropriate in scale for a side chapel could be visually lost on the altar of a vast cathedral.

a Christo. *Surrounded Islands.* 1980–1983. 6,500,000 sq. ft. of floating pink woven polypropylene fabric. © Christo/C.V.J. Corp. 1983.

b Robert Indiana. *Love.* Aluminum. 12 × 12 × 6″ (30 × 30 × 15 cm). Whitney Museum of American Art, New York (purchase, with funds from the Howard and Jean Lipman Foundation, Inc.).

c Edward Ruscha. *Actual Size.* 1962. Oil on canvas, 72 × 67″ (182.9 × 170.2 cm). The Los Angeles County Museum of Art (anonymous gift through the Contemporary Art Council).

a

b

c

Scale Within Art

The second way to discuss artistic scale is to consider the size and scale of elements *within* the design or pattern. The scale here, of course, is relative to the overall area of the format; a big element in one painting might be small in a larger work. Again we often use the term *proportion* to describe the size relationships between the various parts of a unit. To say an element in a composition is "out of proportion" carries a negative feeling. And it is true that such a visual effect is often startling or unsettling. However, it is possible that this reaction is precisely what some artists desire.

The three examples in **a** contain the same elements. But in each design the scale of the items is different, thus altering the proportional relationships between the parts. This results in very different visual effects in the same way that altering the proportions of ingredients in a recipe changes the final dish. Which design is "best" or which we prefer can be argued. The answer would depend upon what effect we wish to create.

Look at the difference scale can make in a painting. Examples **b** and **c** both have themes dealing with the sufferings of Christ. In Tintoretto's painting **(b)** of the crucifixion, tiny figures crowd the scene, and Christ is small in scale, barely identifiable. Tintoretto gives us a vast panorama of events. We see the thieves being crucified with Christ, the soldiers gambling for His robe, the mob—all the various facets of the story. Gauguin's painting **(c)** is in a very different style, but probably the main difference in the two images is the use of scale within the picture. In contrast to the Tintoretto, Gauguin's figure of Christ is large in scale, dominating the whole composition. Here we forget the other events of the crucifixion and concentrate on Christ's sorrows. The mood is sadly quiet as opposed to the exciting activity of the Tintoretto. The "primitive" character of the drawing and the kneeling peasant women give the painting a feeling of innocent simplicity. Both paintings are emotional images, but the scale of the elements results in contrasting impressions.

---

a Changes in scale within a design also change the total effect.
b Jacopo Tintoretto. *The Crucifixion.* 1565. Oil on canvas, 17'7" × 40'2" (5.36 × 12.24 m). Sala dell'Albergo, Scuola di San Rocco, Venice.
c Paul Gauguin. *The Yellow Christ.* 1889. Oil on canvas, 36¼ × 28⅞" (92 × 73.3 cm). Albright-Knox Art Gallery, Buffalo, NY (general purchase funds, 1946).

a

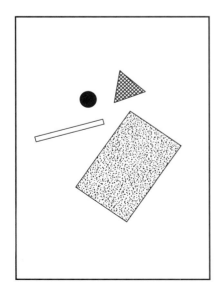 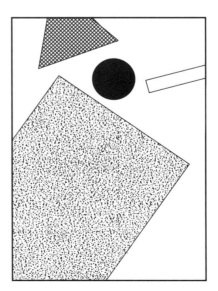 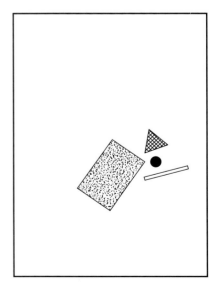

b

c

Scale Within Art

Scale can attract our attention in different ways, depending on the artist's purpose. Scale can also be used to draw our notice to the unexpected or exaggerated, as when small objects are magnified or large ones reduced. The American artist Georgia O'Keeffe took one small blossom of the trumpet vine and enlarged it to canvas-filling scale **(a).** Now a delicate flower fills a canvas 2 ½ feet high.

Painter John Register took the opposite approach to scale **(b).** The small, lone chair isolated in the vast, empty area of the sun-filled waiting room gives a calm but eerie feeling to the composition. Now the deliberate small scale provides the interest.

Unexpected scale is often used in advertising. As visual attention must be directed to a product, we regularly see layouts with a large package, cookie, automobile grille, cereal flake, or whatever. The advertisement in **c** is different. Here it is the headline that is set in bold, almost overwhelming, size. This advertisement was one of a series that appealed for funds to support a local zoo and its animals. The illustrations are carefully integrated with the over-large type (and its use of a phrase used in another context). The visual result commands our attention. Notice that the enormous scale of the headline and pictures is contrasted with the very tiny type for the copy at the bottom. In effect, both ideas of large and small scale are combined. The exaggerated differences in scale create a dynamic design.

a Georgia O'Keeffe. *White Trumpet Flower.* 1932. Oil on canvas, 29¾ × 39¾" (75.6 × 101 cm). San Diego Museum of Art (gift of Mrs. Inez Parker in memory of Earle W. Grant).

b John Register. *Waiting Room for the Beyond.* 1988. Silkscreen, 42 × 42" (106.7 × 106.7 cm). Courtesy Modernism, San Francisco.

c *Save a Few Bucks.* 1987. Advertisement for *Business Times* to solicit funds for a zoo. Anne Goh, Art Director; Victor Lan, Illustrator; Emma Osman, Writer; Ogilvy & Mather, Singapore.

c

Scale Confusion

The deliberate changing of natural scale is not unusual in painting. In religious paintings many artists have arbitrarily increased the size of the Christ or Virgin Mary figure to emphasize philosophic and religious importance.

Some artists, however, use scale changes intentionally to intrigue or mystify us, rather than to clarify the focal point. Surrealism is an art form based on paradox, on images that cannot be explained in rational terms. Artists who work in this manner present the irrational world of the dream or nightmare—recognizable elements in impossible situations. The painting by Magritte **(a)** shows one such enigma, with much of the mystery stemming from a confusion of scale. We identify the various elements easily enough, but they are all the "wrong" size and strange in proportion to each other. Does the painting show an impossibly large comb, shaving brush, bar of soap, and other items, or are these items normal size but placed in a dollhouse room? Neither explanation makes rational sense.

The Dada artists also used irrational imagery. The photomontage in **b,** by Hannah Hoch, again employs scale differences to produce a totally incongruous design. The extreme shifts in size on various parts of the two dancers startle and intrigue the viewer.

An arbitrary change of scale can have another visual surprise. We rather automatically associate size differences with space: Large items are closer to us, while smaller ones are farther away. But the intriguing painting in **c** challenges this size/distance relationship. The painting contains many small scenes. These are all painted in a very naturalistic manner so we can easily understand the images. But, spatially, their relative scale is very puzzling. Due to their sizes, some of these areas start to recede while others jump forward in a disconnected and incongruous manner across the painting. Again a painting with out-of-scale images produces a disconcerting result.

---

a René Magritte. *Personal Values.* 1952. Oil on canvas, 31⅝ × 39½"
(80 × 100 cm). Collection Harry Torczyner, New York.
b Hannah Höch. *Dada Dance.* 1919–1921. Photomontage, 12⅝ × 9"
(32 × 23 cm). Private collection.
c Henry Koerner. *Mirror of Life.* 1946. Oil on composition board, 36 × 42"
(91.4 × 106.7 cm). Whitney Museum of American Art, New York
(purchase).

a

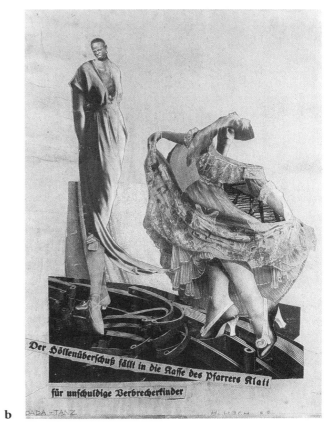

b

c

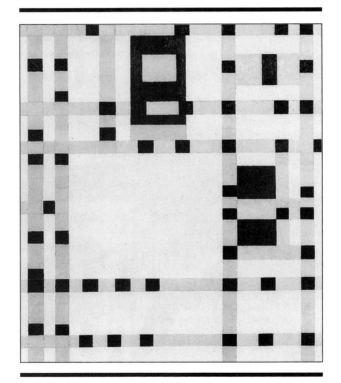

Detail of Piet Mondrian's *Broadway Boogie-Woogie*. 1942–1943. (See page 96 for painting reproduced in its entirety).

C H A P T E R

RHYTHM

Introduction

In conversation we might refer to Bridget Riley's painting in **a** as having a *rhythmic* feeling. This might seem a strange adjective to use because *rhythm* is a term we most often associate with the sense of hearing. Without words, music can intrigue us by its pulsating beat, inducing us to tap a foot or perhaps dance. Poetry often has *meter,* which is a term for measurable rhythm. The pace of words can establish a cadence, a repetitive flow of syllables that makes reading poems aloud a pleasure. But rhythm can also be a visual sensation. We commonly speak of rhythm when watching the movement displayed by athletes, dancers or some workers performing manual tasks. In a similar way the quality of rhythm can be applied to the visual arts, in which the idea is again basically related to movement. Here the concept refers to the movement of the viewer's eye, a movement across recurrent motifs providing the repetition inherent in the idea of rhythm. The painting in **a** has this feeling of repetition in the softly flowing vertical forms. It is not necessarily the nonobjective nature of the shapes in **a** that produces this feeling. A similar effect is present in the photograph shown in **b**. Now tree trunks show the same sinuous and graceful rhythm.

Rhythm as a design principle is based on repetition. Repetition, as an element of visual unity, is exhibited in some manner by almost every work of art. However, rhythm involves a clear repetition of elements that are the same or only slightly modified.

The paintings in **a** and **c** are similar in many ways. Both are devoid of subject matter and present a similar pattern of vertical elements extending across the canvas. But we can sense a subtle difference in the rhythm expressed. The smooth, flowing quality of **a** is not present in the rigid, sharp verticals of the painting by Gene Davis (**c**). The rhythm here seems harder, with crisp elements of stress and pause, almost like a drum sounding an irregular pattern of loud and soft beats.

The senses of sight and hearing are indeed so closely allied that we often relate them by interchanging adjectives (such as ''loud'' and ''soft'' colors). Certainly this relationship is shown in the concept of visual rhythm.

---

a Bridget Riley. *Drift No. 2.* 1966. Acrylic on canvas, 7'7½" × 7'5½" (2.32 × 2.27 m). Albright-Knox Art Gallery, Buffalo, NY (gift of Seymour H. Knox, 1967).

b Albert Renger-Patzsch. *Buchenwald in Fall (or Trees).* 1936. Gelatin silver print, 9 × 6⅝" (22.9 × 16.8 cm). Metropolitan Museum of Art, New York (Warner Communications, Inc., purchase fund, 1978).

c Gene Davis. *Billy Budd.* 1964. Acrylic on canvas, 5'8½" × 6'4⅞" (1.74 × 1.95 m). Charles Cowles Gallery, New York.

a

b

c

a

b

Rhythm and Motion

We may speak of the rhythmic repetition of colors or textures, but most often we think of rhythm in the context of shapes and their arrangement. In music, some rhythms are called *legato,* or connecting and flowing. The same word could easily be applied to the visual effect in **a.** The photograph of Death Valley shows the sand dune ridges in undulating, flowing horizontal curves. The dark and light contrast is quite dramatic, but in several places the changes are soft with smooth transitions. The feeling is quite relaxing and calm.

It is true that the rhythmic pattern an artist chooses can very quickly establish such an emotional response in the viewer. For contrast, look at the painting in **b.** The effect here is also rhythmic, but now of an entirely different sort. Small, bold, sharply dark squares move horizontally and vertically around the light canvas. The shapes are rigidly defined with the value changes sudden and startling. Again, music has a term for this type of rhythm: *staccato,* meaning abrupt changes with a dynamic contrast. The recurrence of these dark squares establishes a visual rhythm. The irregular spacing of these small squares causes the pattern (and rhythm) to be lively, rather than monotonous. The artist, Piet Mondrian, titled this painting *Broadway Boogie-Woogie.* He has expressed in the most abstract visual terms not only the on/off patterns of Broadway's neon landscape but also the rhythmic sounds of 1940s instrumental blues music. The effect for us today is almost like the jumpy, always changing patterns we see in video games.

The rhythms of **a** and **b** are indeed different, but the two examples are also alike in that the rhythm initially established is then consistent and regular throughout the composition. This regularity is not present in Kandinsky's painting **(c).** The eye moves through repeated circular elements, but the points of emphasis are in a very uneven, irregular pattern. We are pushed and pulled in various directions. Our eyes are jerked quickly back and forth across the composition; the rhythm is exciting but also unsettling.

a Bruce Barnbaum. *Dune Ridges at Sunrise, Death Valley.* 1976. Silver gelatin print, 10¾ × 13¼″ (27.3 × 33.6 cm). Courtesy the photographer.
b Piet Mondrian. *Broadway Boogie-Woogie.* 1942−1943. Oil on canvas, 50″ × 50″ (127 × 127 cm). Collection, The Museum of Modern Art, New York (given anonymously).
c Wassily Kandinsky. *Improvisation Sintflut.* 1913. Oil on canvas, 4′⅜″ × 4′11″ (0.95 × 1.50 m). Städtische Galerie im Lenbachhaus, Munich.

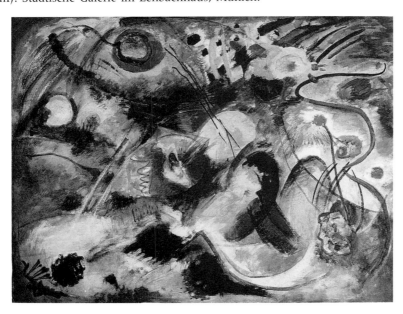

c

Alternating Rhythm

Rhythm is a basic characteristic of nature. The pattern of the seasons, of day and night, of the tides, and even of the movements of the planets, all exhibit a regular rhythm. This rhythm consists of successive patterns in which the same elements reappear in a regular order. In a design or painting this would be termed an *alternating* rhythm, as motifs alternate consistently with one another to produce a regular (and anticipated) sequence. This expected quality of the pattern is not a fault, for unless the repetition is fairly obvious, the whole idea of visual rhythm becomes obscure.

A familiar example of this idea can be seen in a building with columns, such as a Greek temple. The repeating pattern of light columns against darker negative spaces is clearly an alternating rhythm. Architectural critics often speak of the "rhythmic" placement of windows on a facade. Again it is an alternating pattern—dark glass against a solid wall. The exterior stairway of Le Corbusier's building **(a)** shows this type of rhythm. The design involves a sequence of forms that not only alternate in dark and light areas, but shift regularly back and forth from straight edges to curves.

Notice that exactly the same description of alternating themes could be used for the painting in **b.** The artist, Robert Delaunay, titled this work, appropriately, *Rhythm Without End.*

Alternating rhythm is seen, in a less regular way, in Ansel Adams' photograph of Yosemite Valley **(c).** The dark trunks of the trees create a series of tall verticals spaced in an irregular sequence across the format. The areas in between are not empty, negative spaces but are filled with incredibly complex patterns of contrasting, horizontal snow-laden branches.

The same quality can be seen in **d,** a painting by Jacob Lawrence. In this work the tall, vertical, triangular shapes of the train seats move rhythmically across the painting, alternating with the abstracted, generally drooping, tired figures of the train's passengers.

---

a Le Corbusier. Unité d'Habitation. 1947–1952. External escape stairway, Marseilles.

b Robert Delaunay. *Rhythm Without End.* 1935. Gouache, brush and ink, 10⅝ × 8¼″ (27 × 21 cm). Collection, The Museum of Modern Art, New York (given anonymously).

c Ansel Adams. *Pine Forest in Snow, Yosemite National Park, California.* 1933. Courtesy of the Trustees of the Ansel Adams Publishing Rights Trust.

d Jacob Lawrence. *Going Home.* 1946. Gouache, 21½ × 29½″ (55 × 75 cm). Collection, IBM Corporation, Armonk, NY.

a

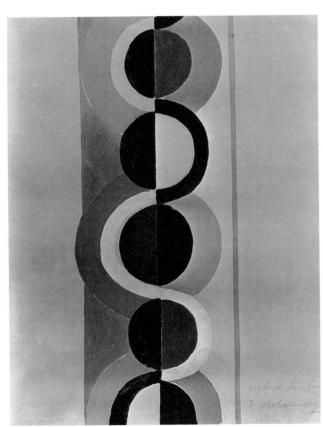

b

Progressive Rhythm

Another type of rhythm is called *progression*, or *progressive rhythm*. Again, the rhythm involves repetition, but repetition of a shape that *changes* in a regular manner. There is a feeling of a sequential pattern. This type of rhythm is most often achieved with a progressive variation of the size of a shape, though its color, value, or texture could be the varying element. Progressive rhythm is extremely familiar to us; we experience it daily. Every time we look at buildings from an angle, the perspective changes the horizontals and verticals into a converging pattern that creates a regular sequence of shapes gradually diminishing in size.

In **a** the rhythmic sequence of shapes moving horizontally across the format is clear whether we look at the white triangles or the black pointed planes.

Both shapes progress regularly from narrow to wider and back again in an orderly rhythm.

The progression of concentric shapes in **b** establishes a rhythmic pattern. Radiating from the small, black, irregular square in the center, the shapes not only grow larger but subtly change to become more curvilinear and rounded as the size increases. All the brushstrokes repeat this same rhythmic pattern.

The photograph in **c** has the same feeling of progressive rhythm seen in **b.** Now instead of a purely nonobjective pattern of shapes, the image is an extreme close-up of an artichoke cut in half. The same impression of repeated shapes gradually increasing in both size and weight is present.

a Francis Celentano. *Flowing Phalanx.* 1965. Synthetic polymer paint on canvas, 34⅛ × 46⅛" (87 × 117 cm). Collection, The Museum of Modern Art, New York (Larry Aldrich Foundation Fund).

b Friedensreich Hundertwasser. *224 Der grosse Weg (The Big Road).* 1955. Mixed media, polyvinyl on canvas, 5'3⅛" × 5'2⅜" (1.62 × 1.6 m). Österreichische Galerie, Vienna.

c Edward Weston. *Artichoke, Halved.* 1930. Gelatin silver print, 7½ × 9½" (19 × 24.1 cm). Collection, The Museum of Modern Art, New York (gift of David H. McAlpin).

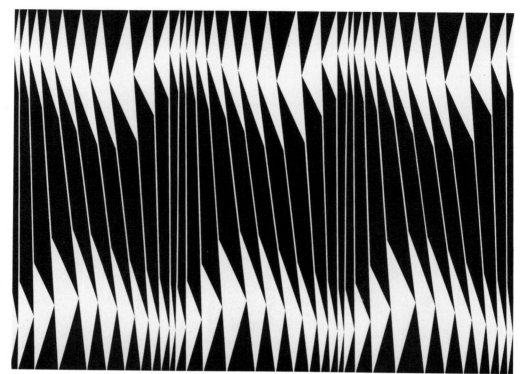

a

b

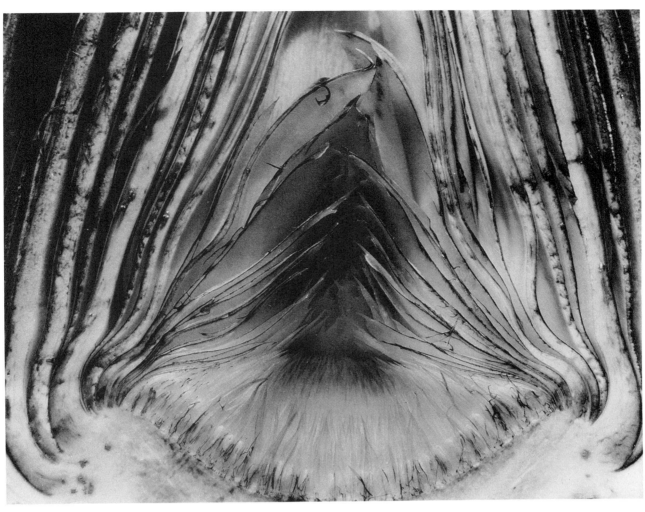

c

LINE

Introduction

Of all the elements in art, line is the most familiar to us. Most of our writing and drawing tools are pointed, and we have been making lines constantly since we were young children. Most of the cartoons we see daily in our newspapers are simple line drawings **(a)**.

What is a line? Other than a mark made by a pointed tool, a line is a form that has length and width, but the width is so tiny compared to the length that we perceive the line as having only the latter dimension. Geometry defines a line as an infinite number of points. The usual art definition of a line is a moving dot. This latter definition is useful to remember because it recognizes the inherent dynamic quality of line. A line is created by movement. Since our eyes must follow it, a line's potential to suggest motion is basic. The impression of movement we feel when looking at the *Dancing Figure* **(b)** shows the idea clearly. The artist's line seems to be moving and "dancing" before our eyes. The rapid, dynamic quality of the line technique expresses the theme of the drawing.

Line is capable of infinite variety. Example **c** shows just a few of the almost unlimited variations possible in the category *line*. A curious feature of line is its power of suggestion. What an expressive tool it can be for the artist! A line is a minimum statement, made quickly with a minimum of effort, but seemingly able to convey all sorts of moods and feelings. The lines pictured in **c** are truly abstract shapes: they depict no objects. Yet we can read into them emotional and expressive qualities. Think of all the adjectives we can apply to lines. We often describe lines as being nervous, angry, happy, free, quiet, excited, calm, graceful, dancing, and many other qualities. The power of suggestion of this basic element is very great.

---

a Gumpertz. *I'm Sorry, Sir, You're Overdrawn.* 1986. © Robert Gumpertz.
b Anonymous Italian. *Dancing Figure.* 16th century. Red chalk, 6¼ × 5¼" (16 × 13 cm). Metropolitan Museum of Art, New York (gift of Cornelius Vanderbilt, 1880).
c Line has almost unlimited variations.

I'm sorry, sir, you're overdrawn

b

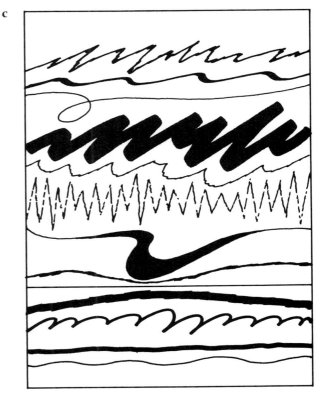

c

Line and Shape

Line is important to the artist because it can describe shape, and by shape we recognize objects. Example **a** is immediately understood as a picture of an apple. It does not have the dimension or mass of an apple; it does not have the color or texture of an apple; it is not the actual size of an apple. Nevertheless, we recognize an apple from the one visual clue of its distinctive shape.

A cliche states that there are no lines in nature. This may be a bit misleading, since there *are* linelike elements in our natural and manufactured environment. Such things as tree twigs, telephone wires, spider webs, railroad tracks, and tall grass certainly are linear in feeling. What the cliche is addressing is illustrated in **b** and **c.** Example **b** is a line drawing—a drawing of *lines* that are *not* present in photograph **c** or in the original scene. In the photograph, of course, no black line runs around each object. The lines in drawing actually show *edges,* while in the photo **c** areas of different value (or color) meet, showing the end of one object and beginning of another. Line is, therefore, an artistic shorthand, useful because, with comparatively few strokes, an artist can describe and identify shapes so that we understand the image.

Line drawings, with the lines describing the edges of various forms abound in art; **d** is just one example. The drawing by Dufy, done quickly with a brush, outlines the many items in the artist's studio with free and loose—but descriptive—lines so that we easily understand the whole scene.

---

a Line describes the shape of a form and helps us identify objects when other characteristics are missing.
b Line, as an artistic shorthand, depicts the edges of shapes.
c Areas of different value delineate the various objects in this scene.
d Raoul Dufy. *The Painter's Studio.* Ca. 1942. Brush and ink, 19⅝ × 26″ (50.4 × 66 cm). Collection, The Museum of Modern Art, New York (gift of Mr. and Mrs. Peter A. Rubel).

a

b

c

d

Types of Line

Line has served artists as a basic tool ever since cave dwellers drew with charred sticks on the cave walls. *Actual* lines **(a)** may vary greatly in weight, character, and other qualities. Two other types of line also figure importantly in pictorial composition.

An *implied* line is created by positioning a series of points so that the eye tends automatically to connect them. The "dotted line" is an example familiar to us all **(b)**. Think also of the "line" waiting for a bus; several figures standing in a row form an implied line.

A *psychic* line is illustrated in **c.** There is no real line, not even intermittent points; yet we *feel* a line, a mental connection between the two elements. This usually occurs when something looks or points in a certain direction. Our eyes invariably follow, and a psychic line results.

All three types of line are present in Perugino's painting of the Crucifixion **(d)**. *Actual* lines are formed, for the edges of figures and background ob-

jects are clearly delineated. An *implied* line is created at the bottom, where the Virgin's feet, the base of the cross, and St. John's feet are points that connect into a horizontal line **(e)**. This line is picked up in the horizontal shadows of the side panels. *Psychic* lines occur as our eyes follow the direction in which each figure is looking. St. John looks up at Christ, and Christ gazes down at the Virgin; this gives us a distinct feeling of a central triangle. Both St. Jerome and St. Mary Magdalene also look at Christ, forming a second, broader triangle. The purpose of these lines is to unify or visually tie together the various elements. Perugino's painting **(d)** may seem static, perhaps a bit posed and artificial, but it is admirably organized into a clear coherent pattern.

Artists should always anticipate the movement of the viewer's eye around their compositions. To a large extent, they can control this movement, and the various types of lines can be a valuable tool.

a There are many types of actual lines, each varying in weight and character.

b The points in an implied line are automatically connected by the eye.

c When one object points to another, the eye connects the two in a psychic line.

d Pietro Perugino. *The Crucifixion with the Virgin, St. John, St. Jerome, and St. Mary Magdalene.* Ca. 1485. Oil on panel; center panel 39⅞ × 22¼" (101 × 57 cm); side panels 37½ × 12" (95 × 31 cm). National Gallery of Art, Washington, DC (Andrew W. Mellon Collection).

e Actual, implied, and psychic lines are all present in *The Crucifixion with the Virgin, St. John, St. Jerome, and St. Mary Magdalene.*

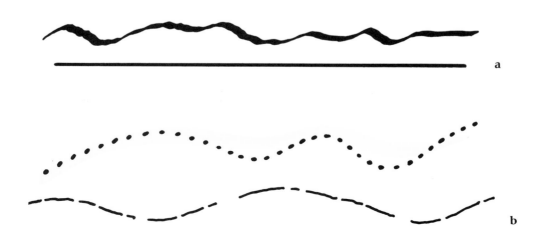

a

b

c

d

e

Line Direction

One important characteristic of line that should be remembered is its *direction*. A horizontal line implies quiet and repose, probably because we associate a horizontal body posture with rest or sleep. A vertical line, such as a standing body, has more potential of activity. But the diagonal line most strongly suggests motion. In so many of the active movements of life (skiing, running, swinging, skating) the body is leaning, so we automatically see diagonals as indicating movement. There is no doubt that we imply more action, more dynamic momentum, from **b** than from **a**. Example **a** is a static, calm pattern; **b** is changing and exciting.

One other factor is involved in the quality of line direction. The outside format of the vast majority of drawings, designs, paintings, and so forth is rectangular. Therefore, any horizontal or vertical line within the work is parallel to, and repetitive of, an edge of the format. The horizontal and vertical lines within a design are called stabilizers, elements that reduce any feeling of movement. The lines in **a** are parallel to the top and bottom, but none of the lines in **b** are.

Poussin's painting **(c)** contains predominantly horizontal and vertical lines, with the diagonal road being the major exception. These lines are diagrammed in **d**. The emphasis, extending even to the clouds, is not just chance. The artist planned it. This painting often is called a *classical* work, a term that implies a static, serene, unchanging image. The emphasis on horizontals and verticals is a major factor in classicism.

The family portrait by Matisse **(e)** could not be called "classical." With its wealth of varied decorative patterns and high contrast of light and dark, it is a very lively painting. But it has a similarity to **c**. The decorative exuberance is contained within a structure of predominately horizontal and vertical lines. The rug and its designs, the fireplace and mantel, the couches, and even the figures themselves show a consistent emphasis on the horizontal and vertical.

SEE ALSO: PLANE/DIAGONAL RECESSION,
PAGE 195.

a Horizontal lines usually imply rest or lack of motion.
b Diagonal lines usually imply movement and action.
c Nicholas Poussin. *The Funeral of Phocion.* 1648. Oil on canvas, 3'11" × 5'10½" (1.19 × 1.79 m). Earl of Plymouth Collection.
d The great number of horizontal and vertical lines in *The Funeral of Phocion* **(c)** suggest calmness and serenity.
e Henri Matisse. *The Painter's Family.* 1911. Oil on canvas, 4'8½" × 6'4¾" (1.43 × 1.94 m). Hermitage, Leningrad.

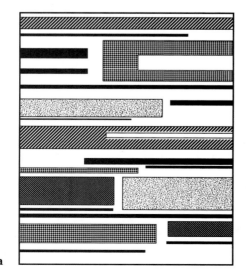

a

b

c

d

e

a

b

c

Contour and Gesture

Regardless of the chosen medium, when line is the main element of an image, the result is called a *drawing*. There are two general types of drawings: *contour* and *gesture*.

When line is used to follow the edges of forms, to describe their outlines, the result is called a *contour* drawing. This is probably the most common use of line in art, and **a** is an example. This portrait by Ingres is a precise drawing with extremely delicate lines carefully describing the features and the folds of the coat. The slightly darker emphasis of the head establishes the focal point. We cannot help but admire the sureness of the drawing, the absolute accuracy of observation.

The drawing of nudes by Kirchner **(b)** is also a contour drawing, but this work has a markedly different character. It obviously was done very quickly, and the line moves rapidly and freely around the bodies' contours. Details are ignored; notice the sketchy quality of the hands. The soft charcoal line suggests the forms in a spontaneous manner, rather than recording exact details.

The other common type of drawing is called a *gesture* drawing. In this instance, describing shapes is less important than showing the action taking place. Line does not stay at the edges, but moves freely within forms. Gesture drawings are not drawings of objects so much as drawings of movement. Because of its very nature, this type of drawing is almost always created quickly and spontaneously. It captures the momentary, changing aspect of the subject, rather than recording nuances of form. Rembrandt's *Christ Carrying the Cross* **(c)** is a gesture drawing. Some quickly drawn lines suggest the contours, but most of the lines are concerned with the action of the falling, moving figures.

In the drawing by Diziani **(d),** the rapid, almost scribbled ink line builds up the figures starting from the gesture of the poses, rather than beginning with clearly defined edges. The artist suggests swaying trees, but we see no definite foliage shapes.

While quite different approaches to drawing, these two categories of line are not mutually exclusive. Many drawings combine elements of both.

---

a Jean Auguste Dominiques Ingres. *Portrait of a Young Man.* Ca. 1815. Pencil, 11½ × 8¾″ (29 × 22 cm). Museum Boymans-van Beuningen, Rotterdam.

b Ernst Ludwig Kirchner. *Nudes.* 1908(?). 13½ × 17½″ (34.3 × 44.4 cm). Solomon R. Guggenheim Museum, New York.

c Rembrandt. *Christ Carrying the Cross.* Ca. 1635. Pen and ink with wash, 5⅝ × 10⅛″ (14 × 26 cm). Kupferstichkabinett, Staatliche Museen, Berlin.

d Gaspare Diziani. *The Flight into Egypt.* 1733. Black pencil and sepia on yellowish paper, 11⅝ × 8½″ (31 × 22 cm). Museo Correr, Venice.

d

Line Quality

To state that an artist uses line is not very descriptive, because line is capable of infinite variety. The illustrations on these two pages give only a sampling of the linear possibilities available to the artist. A similar subject matter has been chosen so that differences in linear technique can be emphasized. The line technique chosen in each case is basically responsible for the different effects immediately obvious in the three works.

Example **a** shows a drawing by Ingres. Like many drawings, this was a study for a later painting, the *Grande Odalisque*. Artists often use the relatively easy and quick medium of drawing to try various compositional possibilities. Drawing **a** is an extremely elegant image. The sinuous, flowing curves of the nude are rendered in a delicate, restrained, light, often almost disappearing line. The actual proportions of the body are altered to stress the long, sweeping, opposing curves that give the drawing its feeling of quiet grace.

The female nude by Marquet in **b** is not delicate in technique or feeling. Here the ink line, done with a brush, is heavy and bold, with variations of thickness. Rather than carefully rendering the body contours, Marquet merely suggests them with a spon-taneous, dynamic line that moves quickly and somewhat imprecisely around the forms. The gray areas in the background, created with a nearly dry brush, reinforce the spontaneous effect, so that we can almost feel the rapid, scribblelike movement of the brush.

The drawing by Daumier **(c)** has a definite theme beyond portraying a woman: It is titled *Fright*. Notice how the line technique conveys this idea. The whole drawing implies movement; we can feel the woman pulling back, recoiling in fear. There is no one contour line. Many lines of varying weight and character (pencil and charcoal) evoke the forms. The hand, for example, is suggested with a few strokes, not clearly defined. Where the contour does emerge, it is built up of repeated strokes. Some lines are mere gesture lines showing the figure's movement. We can sense how the artist worked rapidly, moving quickly over the whole drawing.

The linear technique you choose can produce emotional or expressive qualities in the final pattern. Solid and bold, quiet and flowing, delicate and dainty, jagged and nervous, or countless other possibilities will influence the effect on the viewer of your drawing or design. Choose a theme or decide the effect you wish to impart, and fit the linear technique to it.

a Jean Auguste Dominque Ingres. Study for the *Grande Odalisque*. Ca. 1814. Pencil, 4⅞ × 10½" (12 × 27 cm). Louvre, Paris.

b Albert Marquet. *Nude*. Ca. 1910–1912. Brush (?) and india ink, 11⅝ × 8⅛" (31 × 22 cm). National Gallery of Canada, Ottawa.

c Honoré Daumier. *Fright*. N.d. Charcoal over pencil, 8 × 9¼" (20 × 23 cm). © 1989 Art Institute of Chicago (gift of Robert Allison). All rights reserved.

a

b

c

a

c

b

Line as Value

A single line can show the shape of objects. But an outlined shape is essentially flat; it does not suggest the volume of the original subject.

The artist can, by placing a series of lines close together, create visual areas of gray. By varying the number of lines and their proximity, an almost limitless number of "grays" can be produced. These resulting areas of dark and light (called areas of *value*) can begin to give the three-dimensional quality lacking in a pure contour line. Again, the specific linear technique and the quality of line can vary a great deal among different artists.

The pen-and-ink image of Eve **(a)**—a detail from Durer's *Adam and Eve*—shows a strong contour edge because the light body contrasts with a stark brown background. Within the figure, Durer then added parallel lines in a crisscross pattern (called *crosshatching*) to create areas of gray, which give roundness to the figure. The pen produced necessarily hard, definite strokes, which Durer carefully controlled in direction to follow the volumes of the body forms.

The same pen-and-ink crosshatching technique is clear in **b.** But in this illustration, the artist, Brad Holland, has used the lines in a looser manner, and the areas of gray are now more important and dominant than the outside contours.

Both **a** and **b** use line to create carefully naturalistic volumes and shapes. In the drawing by Henry Moore **(c),** the linear technique is very loose, more spontaneous, and quickly scribbled. The volumes of the figure are now more suggested than carefully delineated. The medium is the same, but the technique is different.

The linocut portrait in **d** uses white lines on black to create areas of bold, crisp patterns. While the various values of gray created relate to the planes of the face, it is in an abstract, schematic manner, and the effect is highly decorative. It is a contrast to the precise exactitude of trying to reproduce appearance found in **a.**

a Albrecht Dürer. *Adam and Eve,* detail. 1504. Pen and broken ink with wash on white paper; entire work 9⅝ × 8″ (24 × 20 cm). Pierpont Morgan Library, New York.

b Brad Holland. *The Observation Deck.* 1979. Ink, 8½ × 11″ (22 × 28 cm). Courtesy the artist.

c Henry Moore. *Half-Figure: Girl,* from *Heads, Figures and Ideas* sketchbook. 1956. Pen and ink, 8⅞ × 6⅞″ (22 × 17 cm). The Henry Moore Foundation.

d *Portrait of Herman Hesse.* 1986. Linocut by Stephen Alcorn for cover of *Siddartha.* Stephen Alcorn, Designer; Club degli Editori, Gruppo Mondadori, Milan, Italy.

d

a

b

c

Line in Painting

Line can be an important element in painting. Since painting basically deals with areas of color, its effect is different from that of drawing, which limits the elements involved. Line becomes important to painting when the artist purposely chooses to outline forms, as Alice Neel does in her portrait **(a).** Dark lines define the edges of the figure, the chair, and the large plant. The lines are bold and quite obvious.

Line can be seen in the detail of Venus from Botticelli's famous painting **(b).** The goddess' hair is a beautiful pattern of flowing, graceful, swirling lines. The hand is delineated from the breast by only the slightest value difference; a dark, now quite delicate line clearly outlines the hand.

Compare the use of line in Botticelli's painting with that in **c.** Both works stress the use of line, but the similarity ends there. *Nurse,* by Roy Lichtenstein **(c),** employs an extremely heavy, bold line—almost a crude line reminiscent of the drawing in comic books. Each artist has adapted his technique to his theme. Compare the treatment of the hair. Venus **(b)** is portrayed as the embodiment of all grace and beauty, her hair a mass of elegant lines in a delicate arabesque pattern. The nurse's hair **(c),** by contrast, is a flat, colored area boldly outlined, with a few slashing, heavy strokes to define its texture. In a comment on North American culture, aesthetics and subtlety have been stripped away, leaving a crass, blatantly commercial image.

The use of a black or dark line in a design is often belittled as a "crutch." There is no doubt that a dark linear structure can often lend desirable emphasis when the initial color or value pattern seems to provide little excitement. Many artists, both past and present, have purposely chosen to exploit the decorative quality of dark line to enhance their work **(d).**

---

a Alice Neel. *Nancy and the Rubber Plant.* 1975. Oil on canvas, 6'8" × 3' (2.03 × 0.91 m). Courtesy the artist.

b Sandro Botticelli. *The Birth of Venus,* detail. Ca. 1480. Oil on canvas; entire work: 5'8⅞" × 9'1⅞" (1.75 × 2.79 m). Uffizi, Florence.

c Roy Lichtenstein. *Nurse.* 1964. Magna on canvas, 4' (1.22 m) square. Courtesy Leo Castelli Gallery.

d Fernand Léger. *Homage to Louis David.* 1948–1949. Oil on canvas, 60½ × 72¾" (153.7 × 184.8 cm). Musée National d'Art Moderne de la Ville de Paris.

d

Line in Painting

Line becomes important in a painting when the contours of the forms are sharply defined, and the viewer's eye is drawn to the edges of the various shapes. David's painting *The Death of Socrates* **(a)** contains no actual outlines, as we have seen in other examples. However, the contour edges of the many figures are very clearly defined. A clean edge separates each of the elements in the painting, so that a line tracing of these edges would show us the whole scene. The color adds interest, but we are most aware of the essential *drawing* underneath. As a mundane comparison, remember the coloring books we had as children and, as we took out our crayons, the parental warnings to "stay within the lines." Despite the absence of actual lines, the David work would be classified as a "linear" painting.

A linear painting is distinguished by its clarity. The emphasis on edges, with the resulting separation of forms, makes a clear, definite statement. Even an abstract painting, which simplifies form and ignores details, presents this effect **(b).**

One other facet of line's role in painting should be noted. Some artists use a linear technique in applying color. The color areas are built up by repeated linear strokes of the brush, which are not smoothed over. Toulouse-Lautrec's cafe scene **(c)** shows this technique. The artist actually drew with the brush; almost every area is constructed of variously colored linear strokes. The line direction varies to describe the different shapes.

Mark Tobey, the painter of **d** also "drew" with the brush. This work shows the repeated linear strokes that create a complex pattern. Here, line is used just as line—not to describe any subject matter. The lines are calligraphic in nature, suggesting the thick and thin forms of brush lettering.

---

a Jacques Louis David. *The Death of Socrates.* 1787. Oil on canvas, 4'3" × 6'5¼" (1.3 × 1.96 m). Metropolitan Museum of Art, New York (Wolfe Fund, 1931. Catharine Lorillard Wolfe Collection).
b Juan Gris. *Guitar and Flowers.* 1912. Oil on canvas, 44⅛ × 27⅝" (112 × 70 cm). Collection, The Museum of Modern Art, New York (bequest of Anna Erickson Levene in memory of her husband, Dr. Phoebus Aaron Theodor Levene).
c Henri de Toulouse-Lautrec. *Monsieur Boileau at the Cafe.* 1893. Gouache on cardboard, 31½ × 25½" (80 × 65 cm). Cleveland Museum of Art (Hinman B. Hurlbut Collection).
d Mark Tobey. *Calligraphy in White.* 1957. Tempera on paper, 35 × 23⅜" (88 × 59 cm). Dallas Museum of Art (gift of Mr. and Mrs. James H. Clark).

a

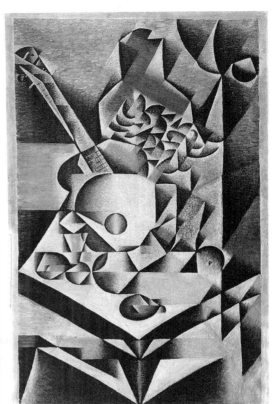

b

c

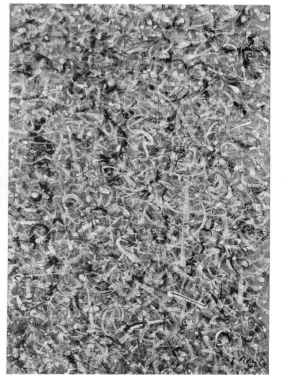

d

a

b

c

d

Lost-and-Found Contour

David's mythological work **(a)** is termed a *linear painting*. All of the forms are depicted with sharp, clear edges. There is no confusion about where one form ends and another begins. If we traced all of the contour edges **(b),** we would have a line drawing that presents the entire scene. The color and value variations of the painting impart a feeling of volume and visual interest, but the line version is perfectly understandable.

The effect is quite different in **c.** This painting by la Tour puts more emphasis on color and value than on line. In each of the figures, only part of the body is revealed by a sharp contour, but the edge then disappears into a mysterious darkness. This is termed *lost-and-found contour:* Now you see it, now you don't. The artist gives us a few clues, and we fill in the rest. For example, when we see a sharply defined hand, we will automatically assume an arm is there, although

we do not see it. A line interpretation **(d)** of this painting proves that we do not get a complete scene, but merely suggestions of form. Bits and pieces float, and it is more difficult to understand the image presented.

A strong linear contour structure in a painting provides clarity. Lost-and-found contour gives only relative clarity, for many forms are not fully described. However, the result is a more exciting, emotional image.

The exciting effect of strong highlights and edges lost in darkness is, of course, not confined to painting. Artists in every medium use it. The photographer choosing the lighting for his subject often exploits the emotional effects of lost-and-found contour. Example **e** is just one of the countless photographs that have used the technique. Here a very beautiful and dramatic image has been produced from a simple architectural detail.

a Jacques Louis David. *Mars Disarmed by Venus and the Graces.* 1824. Oil on canvas, 9'10" × 8'7" (3 × 2.62 m). Musée Royal des Beaux-Arts, Brussels.

b The outlines of the forms in *Mars Disarmed* **(a)** are so clear that a line drawing of it is perfectly understandable.

c Georges de la Tour. *St. Sebastian Mourned by St. Irene and Her Ladies.* 1649. Oil on canvas, 5'3" × 4'3" (1.60 × 1.30 m). Staatliche Museen, West Berlin.

d A line drawing of *St. Sebastian* **(c)** is confusing because the shapes are defined by changing light and shadow, not by line.

e Mark Feldstein. *Untitled.* Photograph.

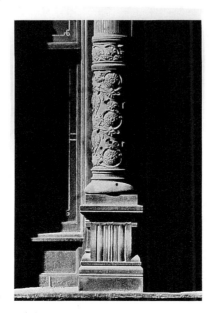

e

CHAPTER

SHAPE/
VOLUME

Introduction

A *shape* is a visually perceived area created either by an enclosing line or by color and value changes defining the outer edges. A shape can also be called a *form*. The two terms are generally synonymous and often are used interchangeably. *Shape* is a more precise term because *form* has other meanings in art. For example, *form* may be used in a broad sense to describe the total visual organization of a work. A work's ''artistic form'' refers not just to shape but also to color, texture, value pattern, composition, and balance. Thus, to avoid confusion, the term *shape* is more specific.

Design, or composition, is basically the arrangement of shapes. The still life painted by seventeenth-century artist Judith Leyster **(a)** is an arrangement of various circular shapes varying in size. Of course, the color, texture, and value of these shapes are important, but the basic element is shape. Historically, line's most important role in art has been to delineate shape. Pictures certainly exist without color, without any significant textural interest, and even without line—but rarely without shape. Only the fuzziest, most diffuse of Impressionism's atmospheric images of light **(b)** can be said almost to dispense with shape.

In designing your own patterns and looking at others' patterns, you must develop the ability to look beyond interesting subject matter to the basic element of shape. The circles in **a** literally represent a basket, a glass, a jug, and various fruits. In another picture, the circle could be a wheel, the sun, an angel's halo, or some other round item. However, the circle's importance in pictorial composition is as a *shape*. In design, seeing shapes is primary; reading their meaning is interesting, but secondary.

Example **c** is a picture created by a computer. The image is interesting because it is clearly a pattern of some 250 squares of various grays and, incidentally, is a picture of Abraham Lincoln. In **c** a midpoint has been established at which we are aware equally of the basic design shapes and the subject matter. Several images were tested to find this midpoint in which most people could see both qualities. When more, smaller squares were used, people saw only Lincoln; with fewer, larger squares, they saw only the gray shapes and not Lincoln's head.

---

a Judith Leyster. *Still Life.* 17th century. Oil on canvas, 26¾ × 24⅜″ (68 × 62 cm). Fine Arts Mutual, Inc., London.
b Claude Monet. *Impression: Sunrise.* 1872. Oil on canvas, 17½ × 21″ (44.4 × 53.3 cm). Musée Marmottan, Paris.
c Spatially organized image of Abraham Lincoln. Blocpix® image from photograph by Mathew Brady. Courtesy E.T. Manning.

a

b

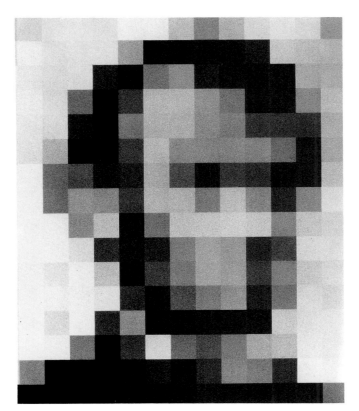

c

Volume/Mass

Shape usually is considered a two-dimensional element, and the words *volume,* or *mass,* are applied to the three-dimensional equivalent. In simplest terms, paintings have shapes, and sculptures have masses. The same terms and distinctions that are applied to shapes apply to three-dimensional volumes or masses. Although the two concepts are closely related, the design considerations of the artist can differ considerably when working in a two- or three-dimensional medium.

A flat work, such as a painting, can be viewed satisfactorily only from a limited number of angles and offers approximately the same image from each angle, but three-dimensional works can be viewed from countless angles as we move around them. The three-dimensional design changes each time we move; the forms are constantly seen in differing relationships. Unless we purposely stop and stare at a piece of sculpture, our visual experience is always fluid, not static. The two photographs of the piece of sculpture by David Smith **(a)** show how radically the design pattern can change depending on our angle of perception.

Thus, in composing art of three-dimensional volume or mass, the artist has more complex consid-

erations. We may simply step back to view the progress of our painting or drawing. With sculpture, we must view the work from a multitude of angles, anticipating all the viewpoints from which it may be seen.

Architecture is the art form most concerned with three-dimensional volumes. Unlike painting or drawing, architecture does not reproduce pictures or models of existing natural objects, but creates three-dimensional shapes by enclosing areas within walls.

A sharp, clear-cut label for art as either two- or three-dimensional is not always possible. Relief sculptures *are* three-dimensional, but because the carving is relatively shallow with a flat back, they actually function more as paintings without color. And many contemporary artists now incorporate three-dimensional elements by attaching items to the canvas. In the work by Tom Wesselmann **(b)** a flatly painted nude dries herself in a painted tub beside an actual shower curtain, bathmat, and hamper. An actual door and towel on the right complete the composition. Many artists today attempt to break down the dividing barriers between painting, sculpture, architecture, and even theater. How would we label a work such as the "installation" **(c)** by the American artist Jonathan Borofsky?

---

a David Smith. *Blackburn: Song of an Irish Blacksmith,* front and side views, 1949–1950. Steel and bronze, 46¼ × 41 × 24″ (117 × 104 × 61 cm); height of base 8″ (20 cm), diameter 7¼″ (18 cm). Wilhelm Lehmbruck Museum, Duisburg, Germany.

b Tom Wesselmann. *Bathtub Collage No. 3.* 1963. Mixed media, 83⅞ × 106¼ × 17⅝″ (213 × 270 × 45 cm). Wallraf-Richartz Museum, Cologne, Germany.

c Jonathan Borofsky. *Installation Paula Cooper Gallery.* 1980. Courtesy Paula Cooper Gallery, New York.

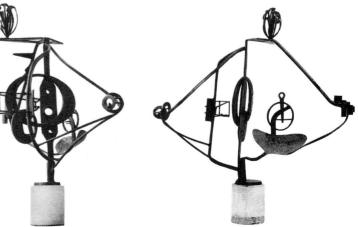

a

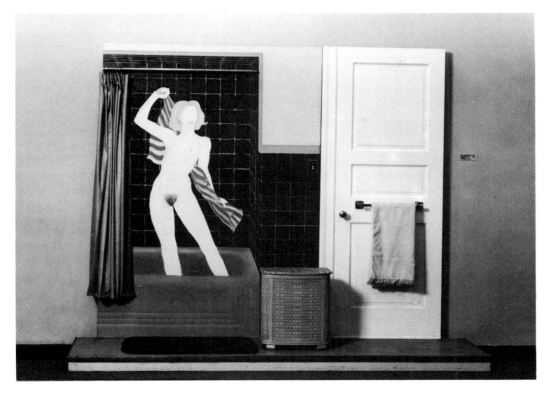

b

c

a

b

c

Naturalism and Distortion

The shape in Eakins' portrait **(a)** would be described as *naturalistic.* The artist has skillfully reproduced the visual image, the forms, and the proportions seen in nature, with an illusion of volume and three-dimensional space. Naturalism is what most people call ''realism,'' meaning, of course, *visual* realism. The radically different visual effect of a similar subject in Soutine's painting **(b)** results from this artist's use of *distortion.* In using distortion, the artist disregards the shapes and forms of nature, purposely changing or exaggerating them. Sometimes distortion is meant to provoke an emotional response on the part of the viewer; sometimes it serves merely to emphasize the design elements inherent in the subject matter.

Many people think that distortion is a twentieth-century development. Now that the camera can easily and cheaply reproduce the appearance of the world around us—a role formerly filled by painting—distortion or its degree has greatly increased in twentieth-century art. However, distortion has always been a facet of art; the artist has rarely been merely a human camera. Distortion of the figures is evident in the eleventh-century illumination shown in **c.** We can identify distortion of size, of human proportions, and of anatomically possible positions. But in **d** the contemporary French sculptor Germaine Richier uses even greater distortion of human shapes and proportions. The grossly elongated forms and sharply acute angles of the limbs take on the attributes of the insect that the title suggests. The lumpy, uneven surface in **d** is a further distortion of the human body. This purposeful disregard of the naturalistic image achieves an emotional and quite menacing image.

a Thomas Eakins. *Miss Van Buren.* Ca. 1886–1890. Oil on canvas, 45 × 32″ (114.3 × 81.2 cm). Phillips Collection, Washington, DC.
b Chaim Soutine. *Woman in Red.* Ca. 1922. Oil on canvas, 36¼ × 25½″ (92 × 65 cm). Musée d'Art Moderne de la Ville de Paris.
c *St. Matthew,* miniature from the Four Gospels. English. Ca. 1040. Manuscript illumination, 8⅛ × 6¾″ (21 × 17 cm). Pierpont Morgan Library, New York.
d Germaine Richier. *Praying Mantis.* N.d. Bronze. Height 4′5″ (1.35 m). Present location unknown. John Cowles Family Collection. Courtesy David Anderson Gallery, Inc., Buffalo, NY.

d

Naturalism and Idealism

Naturalism is concerned with *appearance*. It gives the true-to-life, honest, visual appearance of shapes in the world around us. In contrast, there is a specific type of artistic distortion called *idealism*. Idealism reproduces the world not as it is, but as it should be. Nature is improved upon. All the flaws, accidents, and incongruities of the visual world are corrected.

The self-portrait by Gregory Gillespie **(a)** is naturalistic. Even in painting himself, the artist has indulged in no flattery. If anything, perhaps he has chosen to emphasize the imperfect. The fifth-century B.C. statue **(b)** illustrates the opposite approach—idealism. This statue was a conscious attempt to discover the ideal proportions of the human body. No human figure was copied for this sculpture. The statue represents a visual paragon, a conceptual image of perfection that nature simply does not produce.

Idealism is a recurrent theme in art, as it is in civilized society. We are all idealistic; we all strive for perfection. Despite overwhelming historical evidence, we continue to believe we can create a world without war, poverty, sickness, or social injustice. Obviously, art will periodically reflect this dream of a utopia.

Today we are all familiar with a prevalent, if mundane, form of idealism. Large numbers of the advertisements we see daily are basically idealistic. Beautiful people in romantically lit, luxurious settings induce an atmosphere that is far different from the daily lives of most of us. But yet we do enjoy the glimpse of the "never-never land" awaiting if we use a certain product. Governments also often employ idealistic images to convince the world (or themselves) that their particular political system is superior. The heroic, triumphant figures in **c** are an example. Political propaganda is generally only naturalistic when portraying the opponent.

a Gregory Gillespie. *Myself Painting a Self Portrait.* 1980–1981. Mixed media on wood, 4'10⅛" × 5'8¾" (1.48 × 1.75 m). Hirshhorn Museum and Sculpture Garden, Smithsonian Institution (museum purchase with funds donated by the Board of Trustees, 1981).

b Polyclitus. *Doryphorus (Spear Bearer).* Roman copy after Greek original of Ca. 450–440 B.C. Marble, height 6'6" (1.98 m). Museo Nazionale, Naples.

c Vera Mukhina. *Machine Tractor Driver and Collective Farm Girl.* N.d. Sculpture, U.S.S.R. Economic Achievement Exhibition, Moscow.

a

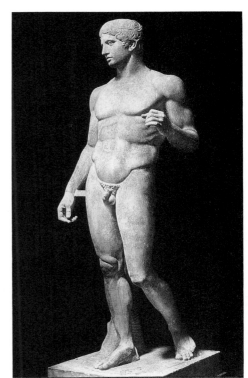

a

b

c

Abstraction

A specific kind of artistic distortion is called *abstraction*. Abstraction implies a simplification of natural shapes to their essential, basic character. Details are ignored as the shapes are reduced to their simplest terms. The child's drawing in **a** is an example of abstraction. It presents a rather complicated scene in a very direct way. Just a few lines describe all the various items in the simplest manner. These few lines constitute the *essence* of the original scene. Exactly the same technique (only in a more sophisticated way) is used in the many comic strips and cartoons we see every day.

Since no artist, no matter how skilled or careful, can possibly reproduce every detail of the natural scene, any painting could be called an abstraction. But the term *abstraction* is most often applied to works in which simplification is visually obvious and important to the final pictorial effect. Of course, the degree of abstraction can vary. In Grant Wood's painting **(b),** almost all the elements have been abstracted to some extent. Many details have been omitted in reducing the hills to simple curving shapes and the trees to circular volumes. Still, the subject matter is immediately recognizable, and we are not too far from the naturalistic image. When the degree of abstraction is slight, as in this example, we often consider the shapes to be *generalized* or *stylized.*

In **c** the amount of abstraction is much greater. These designs were symbols for events at the Olympic Games. At international events, pictorial signs are a more practical communication than words printed in the dozens of languages that would be required. In each of these designs, the human figure in a descriptive athletic pose has been simplified and reduced to a few, extremely simple, flat shapes.

Abstraction is not a new technique; artists have employed this device for centuries. If anything, the desire for naturalism in art is the more recent development. The Eskimo ceremonial carving in **d** clearly shows abstracted forms. Notice how many of the shapes in this mask and also in **c** seem to suggest geometric forms (circles, squares, rectangles, etc.). This illustrates the widely accepted principle: All form, however, complex, is essentially based on, and can be reduced to, a few geometric shapes.

a Mark Odom. *Untitled.* Drawing.

b Grant Wood. *Stone City, Iowa.* 1930. Oil on wood panel, 30¼ × 40" (77 × 102 cm). Joslyn Art Museum, Omaha (Art Institute of Omaha Collection).

c Symbols for the Olympic Games. © 1981 L.A. Olympic Organizing Committee. Courtesy Amateur Athletic Foundation.

d Mask of *Tunghâk, Keeper of the Game.* Inuit (south of the lower Yukon). 19th century. Painted wood, width 36¼" (93 cm). National Museum of Natural History, Smithsonian Institution.

d

Nonobjective Shapes

According to common usage, the term *abstraction* might be applied to the painting in **a**. This would be misleading, however, because the shapes in this work are not natural forms that have been artistically simplified. They do not represent anything other than the geometric forms we see. Rather, they are pure forms. A better term to describe these shapes is *nonobjective*—that is, shapes with no object reference and no subject-matter suggestion.

Most of the original design drawings in this book are nonobjective patterns. Often, it is easier to see an artistic principle or element without a distracting veneer of subject matter. In a similar way, artists in this century are forcing us to observe their works as visual patterns, not story-telling narratives. Without a story, subject, or even definable shapes, a painting must be appreciated solely as a visual design. Lack of subject matter does not necessarily eliminate emotional content in the image. Some nonobjective works are cool, aloof, and unemotional. Paintings such as **a** present purely nonobjective, geometric shapes that are, as Plato said, "free from the sting of desire." Example **b** is equally nonobjective, but the result is highly emotional. The thick paint in agitated, fluid brush strokes forms a dynamic pattern. This spontaneous, restless gesture painting is an exciting creation in pigment.

Whether any shape can be truly nonobjective is a good question. Can we really look at a circle just as a *circle* without beginning to think of some of the countless round objects in our environment? Artists often make use of this instinctive human reflex. A work such as Tony Smith's sculpture **(c)** appears to be a totally nonobjective pattern of forms, yet it reminds us of something. Reading the title *Gracehoper* immediately transforms the image into shapes reminiscent of a giant insect ("grasshopper"). Such reactions, even when not planned, are almost inevitable.

a László Moholy-Nagy. *A II.* 1924. Oil on canvas, 3'9⅝" × 4'5⅝" (1.16 × 1.36 m). Solomon R. Guggenheim Museum, New York.
b Willem de Kooning. *Parc Rosenberg.* 1957. Oil on canvas, 6'8" × 5'10½" (2.03 × 1.79 m). Collection Adrian and Robert Mnuchin.
c Tony Smith. *Gracehoper.* 1972. Welded steel painted black, 23 × 22 × 46' (7.01 × 6.71 × 14.02 m). © The Detroit Institute of Arts (Founders Society purchase, donations from W. Hawkins Ferry, Walter and Josephine Ford Fund, Eleanor Clay Ford, Marie and Alex Manoogian Funds, and members of the Friends of Modern Art).

a

b

c

a

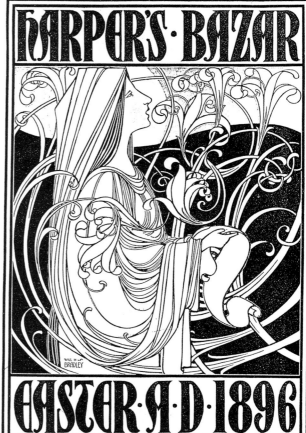

b

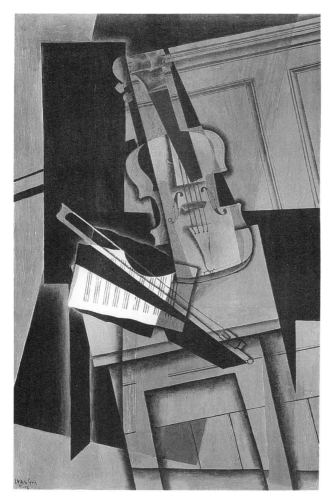

c

Rectilinear and Curvilinear

The title of the painting by Theo van Doesburg **(a)** describes a theme of card players. However, the forms are so highly abstracted that the subject matter becomes relatively unimportant. What we see is a busy pattern of shapes that are all geometric in feeling—with hard, straight edges and angular corners. The term used to describe such shapes is *rectilinear.*

The example in **b** shows an equal emphasis on the opposite type of shape—*curvilinear.* The drapery, hair, scroll and twining lilies swirl around in a design arabesque of graceful curving shapes. Even the letter forms in the titles emphasize the curving forms. This drawing is a product of a late-nineteenth-century style called *Art Nouveau,* which put total pictorial emphasis on natural shapes.

We do think of curvilinear shapes as *natural,* reflecting the soft, flowing shapes found in nature. The term *biomorphic* is sometimes used to describe the same idea. Rectilinear shapes, being more regular and precise, suggest geometry and, hence, appear more artificial and manufactured. Of course, these are very broad conclusions. In fact, geometric shapes abound in nature, especially in the microscopic structure of elements; and people design many objects with irregular, free-form shapes.

Illustrations **a** and **b** concentrate exclusively on a single type of shape. Most art combines both types. In using the two types of shapes, a useful device is to stress one type and use the other sparingly, as a point of emphasis. In the Gris painting **(c),** the table and wall panels make a rigid pattern of sharply defined rectilinear shapes, while the curves of the violin break the angular pattern and create a natural focal point.

The Guggenheim Museum, designed by Frank Lloyd Wright **(d),** also combines the two types of shapes, but the large organic, shell-like curving gallery area dominates the design.

---

a Theo van Doesburg. *Composition IX, Opus 18 (Card Players).* 1917. Oil on canvas, 45¼ × 41⅜″ (116 × 106 cm). Gemeentemuseum, The Hague.
b William H. Bradley. Cover for *Harper's Bazar.* Easter 1896.
c Juan Gris. *The Violin.* 1916. Oil on wood panel, 45½ × 28½″ (117 × 73 cm). Öffentliche Kunstsammlung, Basel.
d Frank Lloyd Wright. Solomon R. Guggenheim Museum, New York, 1959.

d

Positive/Negative Shapes

The four examples in **a** illustrate an important design consideration that is sometimes overlooked. In each of these patterns, the black shape is identical. The very different visual effects are caused solely by its placement within the format. This is because the location of the black shape immediately organizes the empty space into various shapes. We refer to these as *positive* and *negative* shapes. The black shape is a positive element, the white empty space the negative shape or shapes. *Figure* and *ground* are other terms used to describe the same idea—the black shape being the figure.

In paintings with subject matter, the distinction of object and background is usually clear. It is important to remember that *both* elements have been thoughtfully designed and planned by the artist. The subject is the focal point, but the negative areas created are equally important in the final pictorial effect. Japanese art often intrigues the Western viewer because of its unusual design of the negative spaces. In the Japanese print **(b)**, the unusual bend of the central figure and the flow of the robes to touch the edges of the picture create varied and interesting negative spaces. A more usual vertical pose for this figure would have formed more regular, symmetrical shapes in the negative areas.

Negative spaces need not be empty flat areas, as the painting **(c),** by Mark Daily, illustrates. The areas surrounding the teapot and flowers have the same fluid brush strokes and value gradations that define the subject matter. This painting shows another, often unexpected, technique used by many artists. We would usually think of painting the "background" first, and then the foreground objects on top of it. But some artists reverse the procedure. Daily's painting **(c)** has many areas that show the negative area was painted after and on top of the positive.

The same positive/negative concept is applicable also to three-dimensional art forms. The sculpture of Henry Moore is noted for the careful integration of negative space "holes" within the composition. Architecture is, in essence, the enclosure of negative spaces. The contrast of positive and negative areas may also be a primary consideration in the overall design, as the house by Michael Graves **(d)** shows.

a The location of shapes in space organizes the space into positive and negative areas.

b Tōshūsai Sharaku. *The Actor Segawa Tomisaburō as the Courtesan Tōyama Sheltering Ichikawa Kurizō as Higashiyama Yoshiwaka-Maru.* 1794. Woodcut, 13 × 5⅞″ (33 × 15 cm). Metropolitan Museum of Art, New York (Elisha Whittelsey Collection, Whittelsey Fund, 1949).

c Mark Daily. *Brooks Street Peonies.* 1976. Oil on canvas, 20 × 16″ (51 × 41 cm). Courtesy Sandra Wilson Galleries, Denver.

d Michael Graves. Addition to the Benacerraf House. Princeton, New Jersey, 1969.

a

b

c

d

Positive/Negative Shapes

INTEGRATION

Design themes and purposes vary, but some integration between the positive and negative shapes is generally thought desirable. In **a,** the shapes and their placement are interesting enough, but they seem to float aimlessly within the format. They also have what we call a "pasted-on" look, since there is little back-and-forth visual movement between the positive shapes and the negative white background. An unrelieved silhouette of every shape is usually not the most interesting spatial solution. Example **b** shows similar shapes in the same positions as **a,** but the "background" is now broken into areas of value, which lend interest as well as better positive/negative integration. The division into positive and negative is flexible.

The integration of positive and negative shapes is so prevalent in art that innumerable works exhibit it. The most common device is to repeat a color in the positive and negative areas, giving them a visual link.

The artist can also deliberately plan points where the eye will move from object to background. In the painting in **c,** there are several items around the central figure breaking up the negative spaces. But notice that almost no element is completely silhouetted. Instead, there are places where the color of the table, sofa, figure, bowl, and so on, and the background are so close in value that the eye travels easily from one to the other.

With a somewhat similar subject matter, the background in the painting by Matisse **(d)** is broken into rather arbitrary areas of light and dark. These negative areas line up with, and continue the edges of, the positive shapes, but at the same time they contribute a visual variety: The positive elements are sometimes dark against light and at other times light against dark. Matisse's composition is a more sophisticated version of the effect created in **b,** and again the integration of the shapes is achieved.

---

a When positive and negative spaces are too rigidly defined, the result can be rather uninteresting.

b If the negative areas are made more interesting, the positive-negative integration improves.

c William Worcester Churchill. *Leisure.* 1910. Oil on canvas, 30⅛ × 25⅛" (76.5 × 63.8 cm). Courtesy Museum of Fine Arts, Boston (gift of Gorham Hubbard).

d Henri Matisse. *The Painter and His Model.* 1917. Oil on canvas, 4'9⅜" × 3'1⅞" (1.47 × 0.97 m). Musée National d'Art Moderne, Paris.

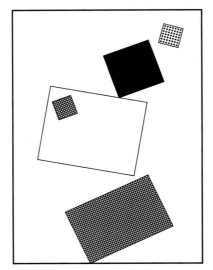

a

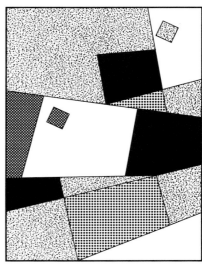

b

a

b

c

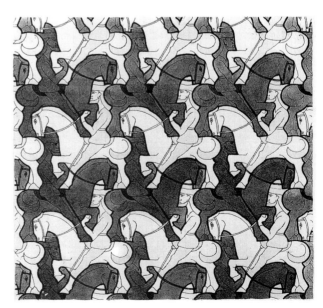

d

Positive/Negative Shapes

CONFUSION

Sometimes positive and negative shapes are integrated to such an extent that there is truly no visual distinction. When we look at the painting in **a,** we automatically see some black shapes on a background. But when we read the artist's title, *White Forms,* suddenly the view changes, and we begin to focus on the *white* shapes, with the black areas now perceived as negative space. The artist has purposely made the positive/negative relationship ambiguous.

The theater poster in **b** has this same quality, as our eyes must shift back and forth from dark to light in seeking the positive element. The first thing we see is a black head in silhouette against a white shape. Then we notice this white area is an outline map of Africa, a map that in the lower right subtly changes and becomes the profile of a young white man. For a play dealing with race relations in South Africa, this design presents both the theme and an intriguing visual pattern.

In most paintings of the past, the separation of object and background was easily seen, even if selected areas merged visually. But several twentieth-century art styles literally do away with the distinc-tion. The viewer's eye can no longer distinguish which shapes are positive and which negative—or perhaps the *whole* area now consists of positive shapes.

Futurism was an early twentieth-century style that attempted to portray the moving, dynamic aspects of the modern world. Example **c,** a painting by the Futurist artist Gino Severini, is a pictorial expression of the constantly moving, shifting visual patterns seen in a Parisian nightclub. The surface of the painting shatters into fragmented images of the scene, suggesting constant movement and change. In the process, any sense of a background of negative shapes is lost, which perhaps is the artist's intent. The *Cubist* artists also created works that had little distinction between the positive and negative elements.

The works of M.C. Escher show the same intentional confusion of positive and negative shapes. With great imagination and brilliant technical facility, Escher creates designs that challenge the whole concept of a distinction between the two types of shape. Example **d** is one of many in which Escher literally abolishes negative space. No matter which color value we focus on in this remarkable design, the shapes appear as positive elements.

---

a Franz Kline. *White Forms.* 1955. Oil on canvas, 6'2⅜" × 4'2¼" (1.89 × 1.28 m). Collection, The Museum of Modern Art, New York (gift of Philip Johnson).

b *"Master Harold"* . . . *and the boys.* 1985. Poster for Department of Theatre Arts, California State University, Los Angeles. David McNutt, Designer; C.S.U. Creative Media Services, Los Angeles.

c Gino Severini. *Dynamic Hieroglyphic of the Bal Tabarin.* 1912. Oil on canvas with sequins, 5'3⅝" × 5'1½" (1.62 × 1.56 m). Collection, The Museum of Modern Art, New York (acquired through the Lillie P. Bliss bequest).

d M.C. Escher. *Study of Regular Division of the Plane with Horsemen.* 1946. India ink and watercolor, 12 × 9" (30 × 23 cm). Escher Foundation, Gemeentemuseum, The Hague.

C H A P T E R

TEXTURE

Introduction

Texture refers to the surface quality of objects. Texture appeals to our sense of touch. Even when we do not actually feel an object, our memory provides a sensory reaction or sensation of touch. In effect, the various light and dark patterns of different textures give visual clues for us to enjoy the textures vicariously. Of course, all objects have some surface quality, even if it is only an unrelieved smooth flatness. The element of texture is illustrated in art when an artist purposely exploits contrasts in surface to provide visual interest.

Many art forms have a basic concern with texture and its visual effects. In most of the craft areas, texture is an important consideration. Ceramics, jewelry, and furniture design often rely heavily on the texture of the materials to enhance the design effect. In weaving and the textile arts, texture is a primary consideration. The soft sculpture in **a** uses a variety of fibers to produce a richly textured piece that is also a weird, macabre image. The interior designer must be sensitive to the visual effects that textural contrasts can achieve.

Architecture today often relies on changes in texture for visual interest. Applied surface decoration has become less important; emphasis is placed on the honest look and "feel" of the materials. The design of the house in **b** uses simple rectangular forms in varying textures. The smooth sheen of glass is contrasted with warm, grained wood in flat horizontal and vertical ribbed patterns. Other areas gain further contrast from the rough, uneven texture of natural stone.

In sculpture exhibits, "Do not touch" signs are a practical (if unhappy) necessity, for so many sculptures appeal to our enjoyment of texture that we almost instinctively want to touch. The smooth translucence of marble, the rough grain of wood, the polish or patina of bronze, the irregular drop of molten solder—each adds a distinctive textural quality.

Visual distance can be a factor in texture. From a distance, many surfaces appear relatively smooth. The closer we get, the rougher and more varied the surface becomes, and microscopic photographs can reveal textural patterns invisible to the naked eye.

---

a Walter Nottingham. *Skins of Us,* detail. 1972. Sculpture in Fiber: Crocheted wool, rayon and horsehair mounted on velvet platform with plexiglass, 1'4" × 5'6" × 2'6" (0.41 × 1.68 × 0.76 m). American Craft Museum of the American Crafts Council, New York.
b Arthur Erickson. Private home, Vancouver, B.C.

a

b

a

b

Tactile Texture

There are two categories of artistic texture—*tactile* and *visual*. Architecture and sculpture employing actual material have what is called *tactile* texture—texture that can actually be felt. In painting, the same term describes an uneven paint surface, when an artist uses thick pigment (a technique called *impasto*) so that a rough, three-dimensional paint surface results.

As the need and desire for illusionism in art faded, tactile texture became a more common aspect of painting. Paintings now could look like what they truly were—paint on canvas. Modifying the painting's surface became another option available to the artist. Van Gogh was an early exponent of the actual application of paint as a further expressive element. The detail in **a** shows how short brushstrokes of thick, undiluted paint are used to build up the agitated, swirling patterns of van Gogh's images. The ridges and raised edges of the paint strokes are obvious to the viewer's eye.

The visual movement of paint strokes—often applied with a palette knife or very large brushes—was an important aspect of many Abstract Expressionist paintings. This technique resembled van Gogh's, but the result was even more dynamic because of the more spontaneous irregular strokes made by the artist. The painting in **b** uses an extremely heavy, rich paint surface created by the thick pigment applied directly with a palette knife. The impression of the paint almost reminds us of frosting generously slathered over a cake.

The dividing line between painting and sculpture disappears in many contemporary works when actual items are attached to the painted surface. The effect is seen in **c.** This is indeed a "mixed media" piece with visual emphasis on the bizarre feathers.

---

a Vincent van Gogh. *Portrait of the Artist,* detail. 1888. Mme. H. Lutjens, Zurich.

b Jean Paul Riopelle. *Vespéral No. 3.* 1958. Oil on canvas, 44¾" × 63½" (113.7 × 161.5 cm). © The Art Institute of Chicago (Mary and Leigh B. Block acquisitions fund). All rights reserved.

c Bruce Conner. *St. Valentine's Day Massacre/Homage to Errol Flynn.* 1960. Feathers, nylon, glass and paper on wood, 19¼ × 14½ × 3½" (48.3 × 36.9 × 8.9 cm). San Francisco Museum of Modern Art (gift of Mr. and Mrs. W. William Gardner).

c

Tactile Texture

COLLAGE

Creating a design by pasting down bits and pieces of colored and textured papers, cloth, or other materials is called *collage*. This artistic technique has been popular for centuries, but mainly in the area of folk art. Only in the twentieth century has collage been seriously considered a legitimate medium of the fine arts.

The collage method is a very serviceable one. It saves the artist the painstaking, often tedious task of carefully reproducing textures in paint. Collage is an excellent medium for beginners. Forms can be altered or reshaped quickly and easily with scissors. Also, compositional arrangements can more easily be tested (before pasting) than when the design is indelibly rendered in paint.

The German artist Kurt Schwitters worked almost exclusively in collage. His *Merz Konstruction* **(a)** shows the visual interest achieved by contrasts of various real textures. The title refers to the fact that these are discarded, valueless items: bits of paper, painted wood, twine, wire, and so on. Schwitters' work makes us realize the design potential of even the most insignificant of materials.

Anne Ryan, an American, worked mainly in collages of cloth. Her untitled collage in **b** shows various bits of cloth in contrasting weaves and textures interspersed with some scraps of printed papers. The dark and light pattern is interesting but our attention is drawn mainly to the contrast of tactile textures.

Working with old scraps of canvas and welded steel, Lee Bontecou created a textural relief that suggests a series of mouths **(c).** The inclusion of zippers in several of the open ovals suggests teeth and somehow gives a very frightening appearance to the whole collage.

---

a Kurt Schwitters. *Merz Konstruction.* 1921. Painted wood, wire and paper, 14½ × 8½″ (36.8 × 21.6 cm). Philadelphia Museum of Art (A.E. Gallatin Collection).

b Anne Ryan. *Untitled, no. 129.* Ca. 1948–1954. Collage on paper, 4¾ × 4¼″ (12.1 × 10.8 cm). Courtesy Washburn Gallery, New York.

c Lee Bontecou. *Untitled.* 1964. Welded steel with canvas, 6′ × 6′8″ × 1′6″ (1.83 × 2.03 × 0.45 m). Honolulu Academy of Arts.

a

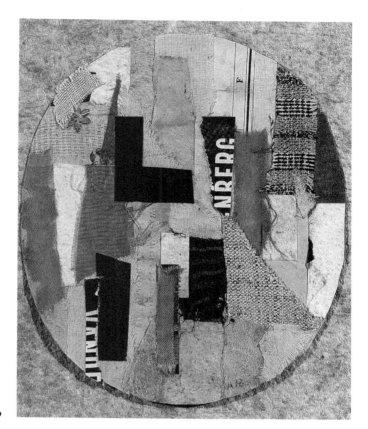

b

c

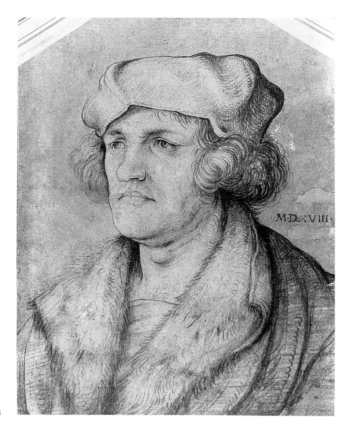

a

b

Visual Texture

In painting, artists can create the impression of texture on a flat, smooth paint surface. By reproducing the color and value patterns of familiar textures, painters can encourage us to see textures where none actually exist. This is called *visual* texture. The impression of texture is purely visual; it cannot be felt or enjoyed by touch. It is only suggested to our eyes.

One of the pleasures of still-life paintings is the contrast of visual textures. These works, lacking story or emotional content, can be purely visual delights as the artist plays one simulated texture against another. Countless beautiful still-life examples exist from many periods of art. Many portraits of the past are interesting today, not because of the identity of largely unknown sitters, but because of the rendition of visual textures: lace, shimmering satin or taffeta, glowing jewels, soft velvet, and so on. The man portrayed in the German drawing **(a)** is not a famous historic fig-

ure. But we look at this today to admire the artist's skill in using black chalk to suggest the textures of the hair, the soft wool cap and the coat's fur collar.

The *Surrealist* artist Max Ernst uses visual texture to help create the eerie mood of his painting *The Eye of Silence* **(b).** A dank, stagnant pool is surrounded by rocks and ruins, all encrusted with creeping, decaying vegetation. The convincing rendering of these textures gives the picture its weird, frightening atmosphere.

Visual texture can also be an interesting design element even without subject matter or any pictorial reference. The work in **c** is titled *Exploration with a Pencil.* The artist created a composition based solely on areas of contrasting visual textures created with pencil and watercolor.

SEE ALSO: VALUE TECHNIQUES, PAGE 223.

a Hans Burgkmair (the Elder). *Portrait of Wolfgang von Maen.* 1518. Black chalk retouched with brush in bistre, 13¾ × 10¾" (35.1 × 27.2 cm). Devonshire Collection, Chatsworth (reproduced by permission of the Chatsworth Settlement).

b Max Ernst. *The Eye of Silence.* 1943–1944. Oil on canvas, 3'6½" × 4'7½" (1.08 × 1.41 m). Washington University Gallery of Art, St. Louis.

c Irene Rice Pereira. *Exploration with a Pencil.* 1940. Pencil and gouache, 13⅞ × 17½" (35 × 44.4 cm). Collection, The Museum of Modern Art, New York (gift of Mrs. Marjorie Falk).

c

a

b

c

Visual Texture

TROMPE L'OEIL

The ultimate point in portraying visual texture is called *trompe l'oeil*, the French term meaning "to fool the eye." This style is commonly defined as "deceptive painting." In trompe l'oeil the objects, in sharp focus, are delineated with meticulous care. The artist copies the exact visual color and value pattern of each surface. A deception occurs because the appearance of objects is so skillfully reproduced that we are momentarily fooled. We look closer, even though our rational brain identifies the image as a painting and not the actual object.

The still life in **a** shows an amusing example of trompe l'oeil. The various portraits and treaty documents are painted in minute detail. These items then appear to be covered by a piece of broken "glass," which proves to be merely painted also. Trompe l'oeil is entertaining for the viewer in this problem of separating reality and illusion.

Sometimes, rather automatically, we associate the term trompe l'oeil only with such nineteenth-century still lifes like **a**. However, this is not true. An interest in this type of illusionistic art has existed for centuries. And this interest has revived today, along with a strong trend back to naturalism in contemporary art. Even in sculpture the trompe l'oeil tradition is alive. The incredibly realistic *Golf Bag* by Marilyn Levine **(b)** is actually made of ceramic, but until one touches or attempts to lift it, the illusion is superb.

The revived interest in naturalism, as a reaction to the abstractions and distortions of the midcentury, has resulted in movements such as *Super Realism*. Illustration **c** reproduces a painting in acrylics, not a photograph. It would be easy to be fooled, however, as every detail is presented with photolike naturalism. The subject is drawn with technical precision and rendered with absolute clarity and exactitude.

It would also be a mistake to think of trompe l'oeil art as confined to painters with tiny brushes laboring over small-scale easel paintings. More and more today in our cities, we are seeing examples of trompe l'oeil art such as **d**. This painting is truly enormous in scale. The entire blank wall of a parking lot has been artistically transformed into a deceptive (and one might think perhaps dangerous) lengthening vista of a seaside road receding under a painted viaduct far into the distance.

---

a Laurent Dabos. *Peace Treaty Between France and Spain.* Oil on canvas, 23 × 18" (59 × 46 cm). Musée Marmottan, Paris.
b Marilyn Levine. *Golf Bag.* 1976. Ceramic on wood board, 35½ × 13 × 6" (90 × 33 × 15 cm). Collection Monroe R. and Leila Meyerson.
c Franz Gertsch. *Making Up.* 1975. Acrylic on canvas, 7'8" × 11'4¼" (2.34 × 3.47 m). Museum Ludwig, Cologne.
d Parking lot mural. 1985. Peter Bresnen. Dartmouth, Nova Scotia.

d

Texture and Pattern

It would be difficult to draw a strict line between *texture* and *pattern*. We immediately associate the word *pattern* with printed fabrics such as plaids, stripes, polka dots, and floral "patterns" **(a).** *Pattern* is usually defined as a repetitive design, with the same motif appearing again and again. Texture, too, often repeats, but its variations usually do not involve such perfect regularity. The difference in the two terms is admittedly slight. A material such as burlap would readily be identified as a tactile texture. Yet the surface design is repetitive enough that a photograph of burlap could be called a pattern.

The essential distinction between texture and pattern seems to be whether the surface arouses our sense of *touch* or merely provides designs appealing to the eye. In other words, while every texture makes a sort of pattern, not every pattern could be considered a texture.

The small intricate designs that dominate the portrait by Klimt in **b** would clearly be called pattern, not texture. While not mechanically repetitive, these designs create decorative colored figures—literally surface patterns—that do not appeal to our sense of touch. The naturalistically rendered body emerging from the ornate, flat, patterned surface provides a startling contrast.

The collage in **c** combines the two ideas in an interesting way. The composition arranges bits of cloth and paper pasted to the surface. So, our tactile sense is involved by wanting to "feel" the various scraps of actual material. But, also, many of these pieces have printed geometric or pictorial patterns on them, so both textural and pattern are part of the final effect.

a Printed patterns often serve as decorative elements in interior design.
b Gustave Klimt. *Adele Bloch-Bauer.* 1907. Oil on canvas, 44⅝" (140 cm) square. Österreichische Galerie, Vienna. © Galerie Welz, Salzburg.
c Miriam Schapiro. *Personal Appearance.* 1985. Paper and acrylic on paper, 7'1" × 6'5" (2.16 × 1.96 m). Courtesy of the artist.

a

10

ILLUSION
OF SPACE

Introduction

Several art forms are three-dimensional and therefore occupy space: ceramics, jewelry and metalwork, weaving, and sculpture, to name a few. In traditional sculpture or in a purely abstract pattern of forms it is important for us to move about and enjoy the changing spatial patterns from various angles. Architecture, of course, is an art form mainly preoccupied with the enclosure of three-dimensional space. A photograph of architecture such as that of the interior court of the National Gallery of Art in Washington, D.C. **(a)** can only hint at the spectacular feeling of space and volume we experience when actually in the area.

In two-dimensional art forms such as drawings, paintings, and prints, the artist often wants to convey a feeling of space or depth. Here space is an illusion, for the images rendered on paper, canvas, or board are essentially flat.

This illusion of space is an option for the artist.

Painting **b,** by Jean Dewasne, is a dynamic pattern of shapes that remain flat on the *picture plane,* the frontal plane of the painting. Nothing encourages us to see "back" into the composition. On the other hand, the Victorian artist Edith Hayller's painting **(c)** pierces the picture plane. We are encouraged to forget that a painting is merely a flat piece of canvas. Instead, we are almost standing in the very room, looking into another, farther room, and seeing the garden through a distant window. Hayller's images suggest three-dimensional forms in an area full of air and "real" space. The picture plane no longer exists as a plane, but becomes a "window" into a simulated three-dimensional world created by the artist. A very convincing illusion is created. Many artists, through the centuries, have studied this problem of presenting a visual illusion of space and depth. Several devices have been used.

a I.M. Pei. East Wing, National Gallery of Art, Washington, D.C. 1978. Mobile by Alexander Calder.
b Jean Dewasne. *La Demeure Antipode.* 1965. Enamel on masonite, 3'1⅞ × 4'2⅞" (0.96 × 1.29 m). Solomon R. Guggenheim Museum, New York (gift of Herbert C. Bernard).
c Edith Hayller. *A Summer Shower.* 1883. Oil on board, 20 × 16¾" (51 × 43 cm). Forbes Magazine Collection, New York.

a

b

c

a

b

Devices to Show Depth

SIZE

The easiest way to create an illusion of space or distance is through *size*. Very early in life, we observe the visual phenomenon that objects, as they get farther away, appear to become smaller. Thus, when we look at the landscape by Hobbema **(a)** we immediately see the relative sizes of the various elements and understand the space that is suggested. The repeating forms of the trees gradually diminish in size and effectively lead us back into space along the narrowing lines of the central road. The tiny figure and small-scale town far in the distance create an impression of great depth. We forget the innate flatness of a picture, and the picture plane becomes like a window glass through which we view a three-dimensional scene.

A difference in size to give a feeling of depth is not confined to formal naturalistic paintings. Saul Steinberg's whimsical lithograph **(b)** uses exactly the same device. Various linear cartoonlike figures and other elements are placed in quite a deep space based on differences in size.

Notice that the size factor can be effective even with abstract shapes, when the forms have no literal meaning or representational quality **(c).** The smaller squares automatically begin to recede, and we see a spatial pattern. With abstract figures, the spatial effect is more pronounced if (as in **c**) the same shape is repeated in various sizes. The device is less effective when different shapes are used **(d).**

---

a Meinhardt Hobbema. *Avenue at Middelharnis.* 1689. Oil on canvas, 3'4¾" × 4'7½" (1.04 × 1.41 m). National Gallery, London. Reproduced by courtesy of the Trustees.
b Saul Steinberg. *Main Street.* 1972–1973. Color lithograph, 15¾ × 22" (40 × 56 cm). Collection, The Museum of Modern Art, New York (gift of Celeste Bartos).
c If the same shape is repeated in different sizes, a spatial effect can be achieved.
d With differing shapes, the spatial illusion is not as clear.

c   d

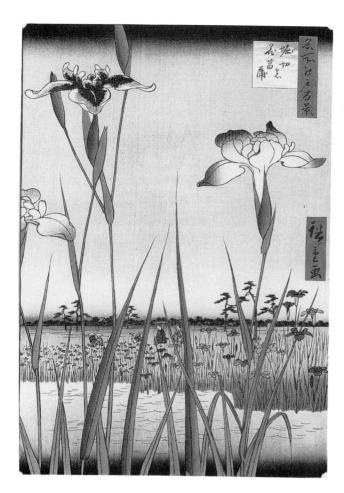

a

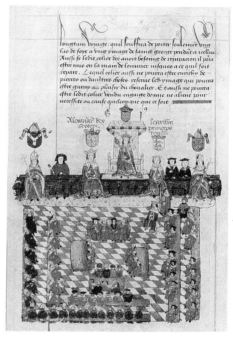

c

b

Devices to Show Depth

SIZE

Using relative sizes to give a feeling of space or depth is very common to many periods and styles of art. Some artists have taken this basic idea and exaggerated it by increasing the size differences. In the Japanese woodcut **(a)** the iris flowers are very large scale and hence seem quite close. By contrast the small trees, tiny figures, and hills seem far in the distance. There are two advantages to this practice. First, seeing some flowers drawn many times larger than human figures automatically forces us to imagine the great distance involved. Second, this very contrast of large and small items can create a dynamic visual pattern.

The theater scene by Degas **(b)** uses the same idea. We have a glimpse of a lady at the far right edge whose large black fan cuts off part of our view of the stage. The size of the central ballerina and the progressive smaller sizes of the other dancers establish the feeling of depth on the stage. Then this very large fan and lady's head extend the feeling of depth to include the theater and audience as well.

In works of art using this technique, a feature such as the flowers or the fan is called a *repoussoir*. The term is not in common use, though the device is often used by artists and photographers.

Artists in the past sometimes ignored size as a way to show spatial location. In looking at the manuscript illustration in **c** we notice that the figures apparently at the "back" of the room are considerably larger in scale than those in the foreground. This is not a mistake or lack of skill on the part of the artist. Often in the past, size was used to denote some conceptual importance and not to indicate how close or far away the figure was spatially. In **c** the figures of the kings and their ministers are portrayed larger simply to show their status as more important and powerful than that of the members of Parliament in the foreground, who are thus in smaller scale. This use of relative size to show importance and not space is called *hieratic scaling*. Although not naturalistic visually, this practice is quite common in art history. Images of gods, angels, saints, and rulers often arbitrarily were shown in a large size to indicate their thematic importance.

a Utagawa (Ando) Hiroshige. *Horikiri Iris Garden* from the series *One Hundred Famous Views of Edo*. 1857. Woodblock print, 13⅜ × 8¾" (34 × 22.2 cm). The Brooklyn Museum, New York.
b Edgar Degas. *Dancer with a Bouquet of Flowers*. Ca. 1878–1880. Oil on canvas, 15⅞ × 19⅞" (40 × 50 cm). Museum of Art, Rhode Island School of Design, Providence, RI (gift of Mrs. Murray S. Danforth).
c *Wriothesley*. Medieval Manuscript. Windsor Castle, Royal Library © Her Majesty Queen Elizabeth II.

Devices to Show Depth

OVERLAPPING

Overlapping is a simple device for creating an illusion of depth. When we look at the design in **a,** we see four elements and have no way to judge their spatial relationships. In **b** the relationship is immediately clear due to overlapping. Each shape hides part of another because it is on top of or in front of the other. A sense of depth is established.

In the detail of Fra Angelico's painting **(c);** the rows of saints are shown with no size difference between the figures in the front row and those in back. But we do understand their respective positions because of the overlapping that hides portions of the figures in the second and third rows. Since overlapping is the only spatial device used, the space created is admittedly very shallow, and we get a "stacked-up" feeling. Notice that when overlapping is combined with size differences, as in Perugino's painting **(d),** the spatial sensation is greatly increased.

The same principle can be illustrated with abstract shapes, as the designs in **e** show. The design at the right, which combines overlapping and size differences, gives a much more effective feeling of spatial recession.

SEE ALSO: TRANSPARENCY, PAGE 196.

a No real feeling of space or depth can be discerned.
b Simple overlapping of the shapes establishes the spatial relationships.
c Fra Angelico. *Christ Glorified in the Court of Heaven,* detail. 1435. Panel, detail 12½ × 25" (32 × 64 cm). National Gallery, London. Reproduced by courtesy of the Trustees.
d Pietro Perugino. *The Delivery of the Keys to Saint Peter,* detail. 1482. Fresco. Sistine Chapel, The Vatican, Rome.
e The design at the left does not give as much feeling of spatial depth as the one on the right.

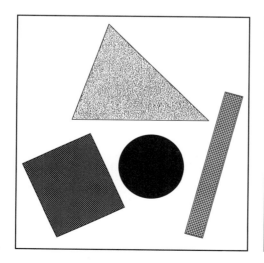

a

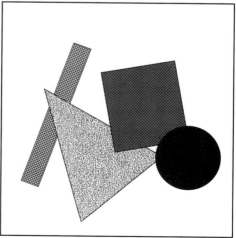

b

c

d

e

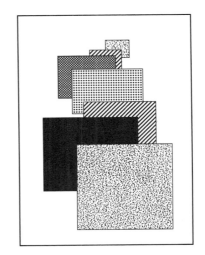

a

b

c

d

Devices to Show Depth

VERTICAL LOCATION

Vertical location is a spatial device in which elevation on the page or format indicates a recession into depth. The *higher* an object, the farther back it is assumed to be. In the Persian miniature **(a)**, the various figures and objects are depicted with no differences in size, but with some overlapping. The artist is relying mainly on vertical location to give us a sense of recession into depth. To our eyes, the effect, though charming and decorative, seems to have little suggestion of depth. The figures appear almost to sit on top of each other all in one plane. However, this device was used widely in Near Eastern art and often in Oriental Art and was immediately understandable in those cultures.

The spatially puzzling American painting in **b** shows the use of vertical location. Again this is about the only clue we have as to spatial positions. There is some overlapping, but the differences in size are very arbitrary; buildings farther away are shown larger than some apparently closer to us. It is only the vertical location placement that enables us even to think of foreground and background.

Vertical location can also be a useful device in more naturalistic art. When the idea of placement is combined with differences in size, an effective feeling of space can be created. In Andrew Wyeth's painting **(c)**, the distance between the figure and the smaller house is emphatically heightened by the placement of the house at the top of the picture. The isolation of the figure is strongly dramatized by the distance created.

Vertical location is based on a visual fact. As we stand and look at the scene before us, the closest place to us is the ground down at our feet. As we gradually raise our eyes upward, objects move further away until we reach what is called the *horizon,* or eye level. Thus, a horizon reference is an integral part of vertical location. In the twentieth century, we have gained the ability to fly, and the traditional ground-horizon-sky visual reference has been considerably altered. We are increasingly accustomed to aerial photographs or "birds-eye" views **(d)** in which the traditional horizon has disappeared, and the point farthest from us can indeed be at the bottom of the picture. Vertical location is still an effective spatial device but not as automatically perceived as in the past.

---

a *Bahram Gur in the Turquoise Palace on Wednesday.* 16th century. Persian miniature. Metropolitan Museum of Art, New York (gift of Alexander Smith Cochran, 1913).

b Joseph Pickett. *Manchester Valley.* 1914–1918 (?). Oil with sand on canvas, $45\frac{1}{2} \times 60\frac{5}{8}''$ (115.6 × 154 cm). Collection, The Museum of Modern Art, New York (gift of Abby Aldrich Rockefeller).

c Andrew Wyeth. *Christina's World.* 1948. Tempera on gesso panel, $32\frac{1}{4} \times 47\frac{3}{4}''$ (82 × 121 cm). Collection, The Museum of Modern Art, New York (purchase).

d Berenice Abbott. *Wall Street, Showing East River from Roof of Irving Trust Company.* 1938. Photograph. Museum of the City of New York.

Devices to Show Depth

AERIAL PERSPECTIVE

Aerial, or *atmospheric, perspective* means the use of color and/or value (dark and light) to show depth. Example **a** illustrates the idea: The value contrast between distant objects gradually lessens, and contours become less distinct. The color would change also, with objects that are far away appearing more neutral in color and taking on a bluish character.

In **b** the feeling of spatial recession is based entirely on differences in size. Example **c** shows the same design, but the spatial feeling is greatly increased, since the smaller shapes become progressively darker and show less value contrast with the background.

In George Robson's nineteenth-century watercolor **(d),** the artist uses gradually lessening value contrasts to establish the sense of the buildings receding farther and farther away. The sharper value contrasts in the foreground figures (boats, stones, etc.) pull these items visually forward. The wall at the bottom left is sharply delineated in detail and value.

SEE ALSO: VALUE AND SPACE, PAGE 221. COLOR AND SPACE, PAGE 244.

a Ansel Adams. *Yosemite Valley from Inspiration Point.* Ca. 1936. Photograph. Courtesy of the Trustees of the Ansel Adams Publishing Rights Trust. All rights reserved.

b A feeling of spatial recession can be achieved simply by reducing the size of objects as they apparently recede into the distance.

c Spatial recession can be made even more effective if the receding objects blend more and more with the background.

d George Fennel Robson. *St. Pauls from Southward by Sunset.* 1833. Watercolor and body color over pencil, 24 × 36" (68 × 92 cm). Yale Center for British Art, New Haven, CT (Paul Mellon Fund).

a

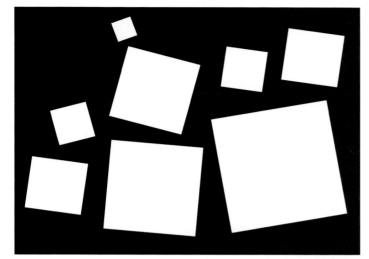

b

c

d

a

b

c

Devices to Show Depth

LINEAR PERSPECTIVE

Linear perspective is a complex spatial system based on a relatively simple visual phenomenon: As parallel lines recede, they appear to converge and to meet on an imaginary line called the *horizon,* or *eye level.* We have all noticed this effect with railroad tracks or a highway stretching away into the distance. From this everyday visual effect, the whole "science" of linear perspective has developed. Artists had long noted this convergence of receding parallel lines, but not until the Renaissance was the idea introduced that parallel lines on parallel planes all converge at the same place (a *vanishing point*) on the horizon. The Surrealist painting in **a** illustrates the idea. The parallel lines of the road, the stone wall and the buildings on the right all gradually taper, leading to one common point. The result is an effective impression of very deep space.

Linear perspective was a dominant device for spatial representation in Western art for several hundred years. It is easy to see why. First, linear perspective does approximate the visual image; it does appear "realistic" for artists striving to reproduce what the eye sees. Second, by its very nature, perspective acts as a unifying factor. With all the lines receding to a common point, it automatically organizes these many trapezoidal shapes into a coherent pattern. The several triangular forms in **a** are visually united by having their angled edges lead to a common point.

Because we look at a corner of the gas station in **b,** the sloping parallel lines of the building would meet at two points on the low horizon line: the right one at the corner of the painting, and the left one outside the format.

Although the introduction of, and continued fascination with, linear perspective as a spatial device was mainly a Western development, examples can be found from other cultures. The Japanese woodcut in **c** is an example. The diagonals of the room's floor, walls, and ceiling are clearly receding to a common vanishing point. The effect here, however, is odd because the figures (unlike **a**) are rendered in very flat, linear patterns and therefore look rather strange in the deep volume created by the perspective lines of the room.

---

a Paul Delvaux. *The Echo.* 1943. Oil on canvas, 41⅜ × 50⅜″ (105 × 128 cm). Aichi Prefectural Museum of Art, Nagoya-city, Japan.

b Edward Ruscha. *Standard Station, Amarillo, Texas.* 1963. Oil on canvas, 5′5″ × 10′4″ (1.65 × 3.15 m). Hood College Museum of Art, Dartmouth College, Hanover, NH.

c Furuyama Moromasa. *Game of Hand Sumō.* Ca. 1740. Woodblock print, 13 × 18½″ (33 × 47 cm). Metropolitan Museum of Art, New York (Frederick C. Hewitt Fund, 1911).

Devices to Show Depth

ONE-POINT/TWO-POINT PERSPECTIVE

The complete study of linear perspective is a complicated task. Entire books are devoted to it alone, and it cannot be fully described here. However, a quick glance at some illustrations and diagrams will enable you to recognize some different perspective systems.

The concept of linear perspective starts with the placement of a horizontal line, the "horizon," that corresponds to the *eye-level* of the artist. On this line are located the needed number of *vanishing points* to which lines or edges will be directed. It might seem that working by a "formula" such as linear perspective provides would lead to a certain sameness and monotony in pictures. This is not true, because the artist's choice in the placement of the horizon and vanishing points on the format (or *outside* it) is almost unlimited. The same scene drawn by the same artist would result in radically different visual compositions by altering these initial choices.

Dirk Bouts' painting **(a)** is an example of what is called *one-point perspective.* A single point has been placed on the horizon line, and all the lines of objects at right angles to the plane of the canvas angle off toward that point. The lines of the walls, windows, ceiling beams, tiled floor, and even the table, if extended, would meet at this common point **(b).** Then, in this created volume, the figures have been placed.

No diagram is needed to illustrate the one-point perspective used in **c.** In this humorous illustration the tiny figure is about to blow up a vast array of buildings. On each of the buildings we can see one side that is parallel to the picture plane, and then the other side diminishes in size as it recedes. The lines of the long buildings here actually recede all the way to the obvious vanishing point.

Though **a** presents a convincing feeling of depth, it might appear a bit contrived as it assumes we are standing still, looking "head on" at the scene. More often, we view objects from some angle, and this is where *two-point perspective* may appear more natural and lifelike. Here no objects are parallel to the picture plane, and all edges recede to *two* points on the horizon. The drawing of a palace's courtyard **(d)** has all diagonal lines, which **e** shows would meet at two common vanishing points outside the format.

Because two-point perspective approximates people's usual visual experience, it is used a great deal in interior and architectural renderings of design proposals.

---

a Dirk Bouts. *Last Supper Altarpiece,* detail. 1464–1467. Panel, 6′ × 5′1⁄8″ (1.83 × 1.53 m). Church of St. Pierre, Louvain.

b The basic structure of the painting in **a** involves all parallel lines converging at the same place.

c Hans-Georg Rauch. *Urban Blast.* 1966. Pen and ink, 17½ × 12½″ (45 × 32 cm). Courtesy of the artist.

d Francesco Guardi. 18th C. *Courtyard of the Ducal Palace.* Drawing, 11¾ × 7⅜″ (30 × 19 cm). Metropolitan Museum of Art, New York (Rogers Fund, 1937).

e The angled lines of the architecture would meet at two points on the horizon.

a

b

c

d

e

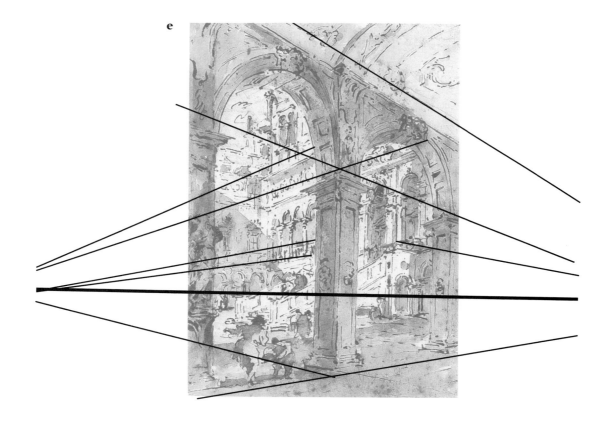

Devices to Show Depth

MULTIPOINT PERSPECTIVE

In perspective drawing, the vertical edges of forms generally remain vertical. Sometimes a third vanishing point is added above (or below) the horizon so that the vertical parallels also taper and converge. This is useful to suggest great height such as looking up at (or down from) a city skyscraper.

Although city streets or a row of buildings might be laid out in orderly rectangular rows of parallel lines, often in real life a variety of angles will be present. This entails the use of *multipoint perspective.* Different objects will have separate sets of vanishing points, though all will still be on a common horizon line. In the painting by Tooker **(a),** the long corridors of the subway recede back at several different angles from the center foreground. Each area thus has a separate vanishing point **(b).** The somewhat threatening feeling of the subway as a maze of confusing passageways is clearly presented.

Painting **c** uses the same idea but in a more abstract and diagrammatic manner.

When the vanishing points of multipoint perspective do not meet on a common horizon line, the impression is that the planes are slanted, inclined, or even floating. The painting by de Chirico **(d)** has a purposely confusing and ambiguous spatial effect. The edges of the foreground planes and background buildings draw closer as they recede, but the vanishing points would be widely divergent. The result is unsettling and strange.

A thorough knowledge of linear perspective is essential for any artist in the many areas of technical illustration and rendering. Painters learn and know the procedures of linear perspective, and countless paintings and drawings employ the basic visual effects. However, today relatively few painters make the preliminary, detailed, perspective drawings that many Renaissance artists appear to have used in creating their paintings.

---

a George Tooker. *The Subway.* 1950. Egg tempera on composition board, 18 × 36″ (46 × 92 cm). Whitney Museum of American Art, New York (Juliana Force, purchase).

b In **a** the angled corridors use several vanishing points.

c Ronald Davis. *Frame and Beam.* 1975. Acrylic and dry pigment, 9′4″ × 15′4½″ (2.9 × 4.73 m). Seattle Art Museum (purchased with funds from the National Endowment for the Arts, Poncho, and R.D. Merrill Foundation; Courtesy of Mrs. Corydon Wagner).

d Giorgio de Chirico. *The Evil Genius of a King.* 1914–1915. Oil on canvas, 24 × 19¾″ (61 × 50.2 cm). Collection, The Museum of Modern Art, New York. (purchase)

a

b

c

d

a

b

Devices to Show Depth

LIMITATIONS OF LINEAR PERSPECTIVE

Linear perspective approximates what our eyes see, but its limitations have made it less popular in the twentieth century than in preceding periods. Many artists object to the restraints that perspective imposes. The artist's compositional freedom consists of the placement of the horizon, vanishing points, and the first line. Then the composition becomes a mechanical drawing exercise in following the rules.

The main objection is the "frozen" quality that linear perspective imparts. With required unchanging horizon line and vanishing points, a perspective drawing suggests a stopping of time; we are staring at a scene without movement. This is not what we experience in life, for our visual knowledge is gained by looking at objects or scenes from many changing viewpoints. Example **a** is a photo of a room from a fixed viewpoint—a "true" view if we would come in, stop completely, and stare at the room without moving our eyes. This, however, is a limited perspective not true to life. In **b,** a composite photo, the camera was focused on several parts of the room successively and the results combined into one composition. This image more closely approximates our visual experience as our eyes move from one item to another, looking at each object in turn.

This changing aspect of perception is obviously what Renato Guttuso has attempted in **c.** Rather than taking one fixed view, the artist shows different figures from different angles to suggest the effect of moving along a beach.

---

a Linear perspective can show only one viewpoint at one moment.
b In reality, our eyes move from one object to another, combining many images to make a composite whole.
c Renato Guttuso. *The Beach.* 1955. Oil on canvas, 9'9⅜ × 14'8¼" (3.01 × 4.52 m). Galleria Nazionale, Parma.

c

a

b

Amplified Perspective

To introduce a dramatic, dynamic quality into their pictures, many artists have used what is called *amplified perspective*. This device reproduces the visual image, but in the very special view that occurs when an item is pointed directly at the viewer.

A familiar example is the old army recruiting poster, where Uncle Sam's pointing finger is thrust forward (''I want you'') and right at the viewer. The same effect can be seen in **a,** in which Sherlock Holmes points right at us, as his arm recedes sharply. This effect is called *foreshortening*. Because the arm points right at us, it looks shorter than we know it to be. In profile, of course, the arm would look much longer.

In Dali's painting of the Crucifixion **(b),** the body of Christ is also foreshortened. We look from above the cross so that the body very quickly recedes down and away from us, rapidly getting smaller. It is an unusual view, and the size contrast of large to small is pictorially exciting.

The same contrast of size can be seen in Andrew Wyeth's painting in **c.** The tree trunk points at us in large scale, receding almost immediately to the forest floor, where we see the tiny figure of the hunter. An advantage of amplified perspective is that the viewer's eye is pulled quickly into the picture. In **c,** from the close tree branches to the far figure exerts a dynamic pull inward, avoiding the static, frozen quality of so many works. With amplified perspective, the spatial quality becomes the image's most eye-catching element. It is an effective tool for making the viewer forget that the picture is a flat, two-dimensional plane.

---

a *The Adventures of Sherlock Holmes Series I.* © 1985 Paul Davis/© 1985 Mobil Corporation. Poster for Mobil Corp.'s Mystery Series on PBS. Paul Davis, Art Director and Designer. Paul Davis Studio. Posters made possible by a grant from Mobil Corp. © 1988.

b Salvador Dali. *Christ of St. John of the Cross.* 1951. Oil on canvas, 6'8⅝ × 3'9⅝" (2.05 × 1.16 m). Glasgow Art Gallery and Museum (purchase, 1952).

c Andrew Wyeth. *The Hunter.* 1943. Tempera on wood panel, 33 × 33⅞" (84 × 86 cm). Toledo Museum of Art (Elizabeth C. Mau Bequest Fund).

c

Multiple Perspective

Looking at a figure or object from more than one vantage point simultaneously is called *multiple perspective.* Several different views are combined in one image. This device has been used widely in twentieth-century art, although the idea is centuries old.

Multiple perspective was a basic pictorial device in Egyptian art, as illustrated in a typical Egyptian painted figure **(a).** The artist's aim was not necessarily to reproduce the visual image, but to give a composite image combining the most descriptive or characteristic view of each part of the body. In **b,** which view of the head is most descriptive, which most certainly a head? The profile obviously says "head" more clearly. But what about the eye **(c)?** The eye in profile is a confusing shape, but the front view is what we know as an eye. The Egyptians solved this problem by combining a side view of the head with a front view of the eye. Each body part is thus presented in its most characteristic aspect: a front view of the torso, a side view of the legs, and so forth.

Much the same reasoning probably inspired the nineteenth-century American artist in the charming drawing of a Pennsylvania farm **(d).** Fields, barn, house, orchard, and so on, are seen from different viewpoints, but each presents the clearest, most typical aspect.

In the twentieth century, with the camera able to give us effortlessly the fixed visual ("realistic") view, artists have been freed to explore other avenues of perception including multiple perspective. The Cubist artist Braque clearly employed multiple perspective in his still life **(e).** We look down on the top of the table to see more clearly the items collected there. But the table is as important as the objects (the picture is entitled *The Round Table*), and it would be a pity not to see the delightful old-fashioned base and curved legs. So we see them from the side. The items themselves, while *abstracted* or simplified into basic shapes, are shown from differing angles to give us the most descriptive view of each individual item.

As you have noticed, multiple perspective does not give a clear spatial pattern of the position occupied by each element. This aspect has been sacrificed to give a more subjective, conceptual view of forms.

a *The Sculptor Ipuy and His Wife,* detail of Egyptian wall painting (restored). Ca. 1275 B.C. Tomb of Ipuy, Deir el Medina. Metropolitan Museum of Art, New York.

b To the Egyptians, the head shown in profile seemed to be the most characteristic view.

c The front view of the eye gives the clearest, most descriptive view.

d Anonymous. *Pennsylvania Farmstead with Many Fences.* Ca. 1830. Pen and watercolor, 18 × 23⅞″ (45 × 59.6 cm). Courtesy Museum of Fine Arts, Boston (M. and M. Karolik Collection).

e Georges Braque. *The Round Table (Le Grand Gueridon).* 1929. Oil on canvas, 4′9¼″ × 3′8¾″ (1.45 × 1.14 m). Phillips Collection, Washington, DC.

a

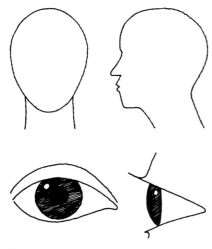

Isometric Projection

For centuries, Oriental artists did not make wide use of linear perspective. Another spatial convention was satisfactory for their pictorial purposes. In Oriental art, planes recede on the diagonal, but the lines, instead of drawing closer together, remain parallel. Example **a** shows a box drawn in linear perspective; **b** shows the box drawn in the Oriental method. In the West, we refer to image **b** as an *isometric projection.*

A typical Japanese print **(c)** illustrates this device. The effect is different, but certainly not disturbing. For one thing, the space is already very shallow; the back of the area is not far from the picture plane. The rather flat decorative effect seems perfectly in keeping with the treatment of the figures, with their strong linear pattern and flat color areas. The artist does not stress three-dimensional solidity or roundness in the figures, so we do not miss this quality in the background. Oriental art rarely stressed the strictly visual impression of the world. The art was more subjective, more evocative than descriptive of the natural world. Linear perspective was undoubtedly not needed for the expressive aims of these artists.

Isometric projection, while used extensively in engineering and mechanical drawings, is rarely seen in Western painting. The self-portrait by David Hockney **(d)** uses this device, and the change from the linear perspective is fresh and intriguing.

The work by Josef Albers **(e)** uses this idea in a purely abstract way. The artist creates a geometric shape drawn in an isometric-type view. The interesting aspect of the design, however, is the shifting, puzzling spatial pattern that emerges. The direction of any plane seems to advance, then recede, then to be flat in a fascinating ambiguity.

---

a In linear perspective, parallel lines gradually draw closer together as they recede into the distance.

b In isometric projection, parallel lines remain parallel.

c Torii Kiyomasu I. *An Oiran with Two Kamuro Stopping in the Street.* Ca. 1690–1710. Japanese print, 11 × 16" (28 × 41 cm). Metropolitan Museum of Art, New York (Harris Brisbane Dick Fund, 1949).

d David Hockney. *Self-Portrait with Blue Guitar.* 1977. Oil on canvas, 5' × 6' (1.52 × 1.83 m). Collection Dr. Peter Ludwig, Aachen.

e Josef Albers. *Structural Constellation II.* Ca. 1950. Machine-engraved vinylite mounted on board, 17 × 22½" (43.2 × 57.1 cm). Collection, The Josef Albers Foundation.

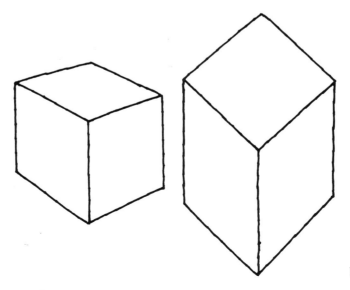

a   b

c

d

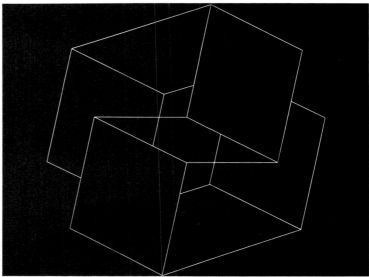

e

a

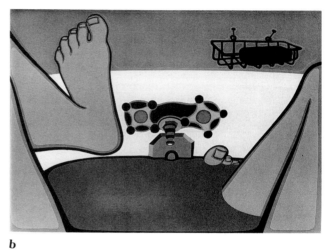

b

c

Open Form/Closed Form

One other aspect of pictorial space is of concern to the artist or designer. This is the concept of *enclosure,* the use of what is referred to as *open form* or *closed form.* The artist has the choice of giving us a complete scene or merely a partial glimpse of a portion of a scene that continues beyond the format. In **a,** Bellini puts the focal point in the center of the composition, and our eyes are not led out of the painting. The Madonna is "framed" effectively by the inward-facing figures on either side, the vertical ornate pillars at the far edges, the downward curving architectural cornice at the top, and even the triangular group of angelic musicians at the bottom. Wherever we look our attention is directed back to the Madonna. This is called *closed form.*

By contrast, example **b** is clearly *open form.* In Clayton Pond's humorous serigraph, only partial glimpses of the figure are seen, and all these lead the eye *off* the format. In fact, this design almost forces us to think more of the parts we *cannot* see than of those shown in the picture.

The ultimate extension of the open form concept is illustrated in **c.** This mixed media painting has actual pieces of cloth and rope draped on the painted surface. These elements then extend outside the rectangular format and effectively destroy any framed, or contained, feeling.

We do generally frame paintings; a frame is a border around the perimeter that visually turns the eye inward. Thus, frames create the effect of closed form, no matter what the original design of the artwork. Some artists have gone even further and included painted "frames" (and even lettered titles) as elements within the composition **(d).**

As you can see, closed form generally gives a rather formal, structured appearance, whereas open form creates a casual, momentary feeling, with elements moving on and off the format in an informal manner.

---

a Giovanni Bellini. *Madonna and Child Enthroned (San Giobbe Altarpiece).* Ca. 1485. Panel, 15'4" × 8'4" (4.67 × 2.54 m). Accademia, Venice.
b Clayton Pond. *Self-Portrait in the Bathtub,* from the series *Things in My Studio.* 1973. Screenprint, 23 × 29" (58 × 74 cm). Courtesy Associated American Artists, New York.
c Antoni Tàpies. *Painting with Cloth and Rope.* 1975. Mixed media on plywood, 71 × 63¾" (178 × 170 cm). David Anderson Gallery, Buffalo, NY.
d Neil Jenny. *North America Abstracted.* 1980. Oil on wood, 3'1¼" × 7'1¼" (0.92 × 2.17 m). Whitney Museum of American Art, New York (purchase).

d

a

b

c

Recession

PLANE/DIAGONAL RECESSION

In discussing pictorial space, one more concept must be mentioned. *How* does the recession into depth occur?

There are two basic devices. *Plane recession* shows distance by receding on a series of planes that are parallel to the picture plane. Recession is, therefore, slow and orderly; most of the movement is side to side or up and down. *Diagonal recession* occurs when the planes are not flat but recede diagonally on an angle, rapidly opening up the pictorial space. The movement is now back and forth or in and out. We are not discussing the degree of depth—how "deep" or "shallow" the picture is—but just *how* the recession is achieved.

In Mary Cassatt's etching **(a),** the figures being mainly line-drawn are somewhat flat and create a horizontal plane in front of the flat wall and windows of the bus. In the distance a bridge makes another parallel plane. The plane recession is clear.

Caillebotte's scene of a Parisian bridge **(b)** is entirely different. The emphasis here is on diagonals.

The steel bridge girders and the side street at the left recede quickly into the distance. The eye is "pulled" rapidly and dramatically into a very deep space. The position of the figures reinforces the diagonal movement. The distance here may not be greater, but the feeling of depth is emphasized.

Though its artist was not trying for the illusion of great distance achieved in **b,** the painting by Edward Hopper **(c)** shows the same diagonal recession. The front counter recedes sharply, with the row of light-colored oranges emphasizing the diagonal. The cashier's stand and the tables recede on a less acute angle to the left, an angle repeated in the tiled floor. Some fruit in the foreground, the waitress's extended arm and head, and the background diner's head also give a more subtle front-to-back diagonal movement.

Although plane recession is less dramatic, it is not necessarily dull or lifeless. The *Circus Parade* **(d)** uses plane recession, yet even though the painting remains relatively flat, the host of decorative patterns and the contrasts of value make it a lively, active picture.

---

a Mary Stevenson Cassatt. *In the Omnibus.* 1891. Drypoint and aquatint, 14½ × 10½" (36.2 × 27 cm). The Carnegie Museum of Art, Pittsburgh, PA (Leisser Art Fund, 1950).

b Gustave Caillebotte. *Le Pont de l'Europe.* 1876. Oil on canvas, 49⅛ × 71⅛" (124.7 × 180.6 cm). Musee du Petit Palais, Geneva.

c Edward Hopper. *Tables for Ladies.* 1930. Oil on canvas, 48¼ × 60¼" (102.2 × 153 cm). Metropolitan Museum of Art, New York (George A. Hearn Fund, 1931).

d Cathy Jacobson. *Circus Parade.* 1979. Oil on canvas, 24 × 36" (61 × 91.4 cm). Museum of American Folk Art (gift of Robert Bishop).

d

Transparency

EQUIVOCAL SPACE

With the camera able to reproduce images easily and quickly, much art in the twentieth century has not been concerned with a purely naturalistic reproduction of the world around us. This is true in the area of spatial and depth representation also. Many artists have chosen to ignore the device of overlapping. Instead, they have used what is called *transparency*. When two forms overlap and both are seen completely, the figures are assumed to be "transparent" **(a)**.

Transparency does *not* give us a clear spatial pattern. In **a** we are not sure which form is on top and which behind. The spatial pattern can change as we look at it. This purposeful ambiguity is called *equivocal space,* and many artists find it a more interesting visual pattern than the immediately clear spatial organization provided by overlapping in a design.

There is another rationale for the use of transparency. Just because one item is in front and hides another object does not mean the item in back has ceased to exist. In **b** a bowl of fruit is depicted with the customary visual device of overlapping. In **c** the same bowl of fruit is shown with transparency, and we discover that other pieces of fruit are in the bottom of the bowl. They were always there, but hidden from our view. Which design is more "realistic"? By what standard do you decide?

Cubism was an art style primarily interested in studying form. Cubist artists often used transparency **(d)** because they felt the contrast and relationship of various shapes was more effective when each was seen entirely, instead of being partially hidden by the momentary accident of overlapping.

The screenprint by Andy Warhol **(e)** is an arrangement of one image (the familiar *Mona Lisa*) repeated in various sizes. Spatial interest is increased by using transparency in many places so the forms interpenetrate rather than get hidden by the more usual overlapping technique.

---

a The use of overlapping with transparency confuses our perception of depth.

b Overlapping sometimes can be deceptive.

c The use of transparency reveals what is hidden by overlapping.

d Juan Gris. *Still Life Before an Open Window: Place Ravignan.* 1915. Oil on canvas, 44¾ × 35" (114 × 89 cm). Philadelphia Museum of Art (Louise and Walter Arensberg Collection).

e Andy Warhol. *Colored Mona Lisa.* 1963. Screenprint on canvas, 10'8" × 6'10" (3.25 × 2.08 m). Copyright © 1989 The Estate and Foundation of Andy Warhol.

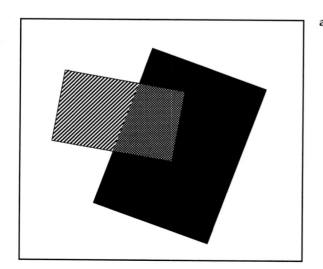

a

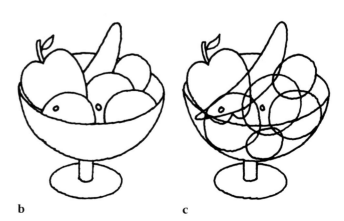

b   c

d

e

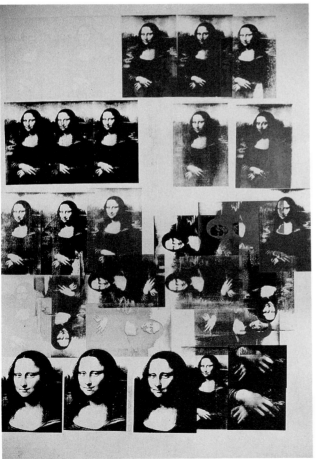

Spatial Puzzles

Artists all have learned the various devices to give an illusion of depth or space. At times, certain artists purposely ignore these conventions to provide an unexpected image. A confusion of spatial relationships is intriguing because the viewer is confronted with a visual puzzle rather than a statement.

Piranesi, in one of his many etchings of prisons **(a),** not only ignores the "rules" but actually distorts them to create a weird, spatially intricate scene. The confused, mazelike complexity of the enormous chamber serves as an ominous symbol of government bureaucracy and repression.

Example **b** is a Surrealist painting. The whole thrust of Surrealism was to illustrate the impossible world of dreams and the subconscious mind. In **b**

René Magritte gives us a truly strange painting. We are outside a building looking in a window, and the scene *inside* is another exterior. There is no way to explain this logically; we experience a strange visual paradox.

M.C. Escher has produced many works that purposely employ this confusion of spatial relationships. His work is fascinating as, at first glance, the careful rendering and brilliant draftsmanship seem to present a perfectly straightforward scene. The lithograph *Belvedere* **(c)** is an example. However, look closely at the columns on the building. Now, suddenly the supposedly normal scene becomes a puzzling, impossible spatial situation.

a Giovanni Battista Piranesi. *The Prisons.* Ca. 1750. Etching, 21⅜ × 16¼" (54 × 41 cm). Metropolitan Museum of Art, New York (Harris Brisbane Dick Fund, 1937).

b René Magritte. *In Praise of Dialectics.* 1937. Oil on canvas, 25⅛ × 21" (64.5 × 54 cm). National Gallery of Victoria, Melbourne, Australia (Felton Bequest, 1971).

c M.C. Escher. *Belvedere.* 1958. Lithograph, 18⅛ × 11⅝" (46.1 × 29.5 cm). © 1989 M.C. Escher Heirs/Cordon Art, Baarn, The Netherlands

a

b

c

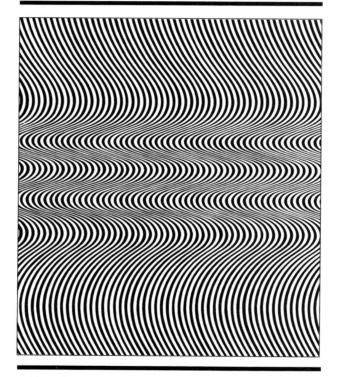

Bridget Riley. *Current,* "detail." 1964. Synthetic polymer paint on composition board, 4'10 3/8" × 4'10 7/8" (1.48 × 1.50m). Collection, The Museum of Modern Art, New York (Philip Johnson Fund).

ILLUSION OF MOTION

Introduction

Change and movement are basic characteristics of existence. Our world is a world of movement. Almost every aspect of life involves constant change. We humans cannot sit or stand motionless for more than a moment or so; even in sleep we turn and change position. But if we could stop our body movements, the world about us would still continue to change. Thus motion is an important consideration in art.

In any of the three-dimensional arts, such as sculpture and architecture, much of the observer's visual pleasure has come from moving about and looking at the work from different angles. But some art forms themselves move, and we apply the term *kinetic* to them. Kinetic sculpture moves, although we may stand still. Although not unknown in history, the idea of kinetic sculpture has become increasingly important in the past few decades. We are all familiar with mobiles, hanging constructions of shapes and wires that are designed to turn and revolve, presenting a constantly changing visual pattern. The relationship of the shapes is always shifting and creating new designs. Today many sculptures have motors, blinking lights, and other moving parts to present this art-in-motion concept. The sculpture in **a** combines the idea of a machine with the pleasures of a fountain of flowing water. Various abstract volumes fill with water, then overturn (spilling the water), and begin to fill again. A constantly changing and moving design is intriguing to watch.

Only the movies or television can actually show us "moving pictures." In paintings or drawings that are static images, any feeling of motion or change is always merely a suggestion or an illusion. This illusion, however, has intrigued artists of many periods and countries.

The paintings shown in **b** and **c** have a great many visual differences. But they both are twentieth-century attempts to present this feeling of motion. In the painting by de Kooning **(b)**, our eyes dart rapidly around the canvas following the complicated pattern of the vigorous, spontaneous brush strokes. This is an example of *Abstract Expressionism* (also called "Action Painting," an apt description, for we can sense the physical activity of the artist in creating the painting). This style has movement and dynamic excitement as primary goals.

Bridget Riley's painting, **(c)**, shows a very different technique. It is a very controlled, simply repetitive pattern of very definite, hard-edged curving lines. But when we stare at it, the edges begin to blur and the lines begin to "swim," as the black and white areas vibrate. Even the painting's surface appears no longer flat, but seems to undulate and become a rippling surface. This type of painting is called "Op Art," images that give optical illusions of movement in static images.

Two paintings quite dissimilar in style have the same goal—an illusion of motion.

---

a Lin Emery. *Homage to Amercreo.* 1964. Wood, height 6′8″ (2.03 m). American Creosote Works, Inc., New Orleans.

b Willem de Kooning. *Composition.* 1955. Oil, enamel and charcoal on canvas, 6′7⅛″ × 5′9⅛″ (2.01 × 1.76 m). Solomon R. Guggenheim Museum, New York.

c Bridget Riley. *Current.* 1964. Synthetic polymer paint on canvas, 4′10⅜″ × 4′10⅞″ (1.48 × 1.5 m). Collection, The Museum of Modern Art, New York (Philip Johnson Fund).

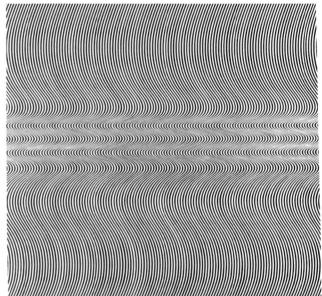

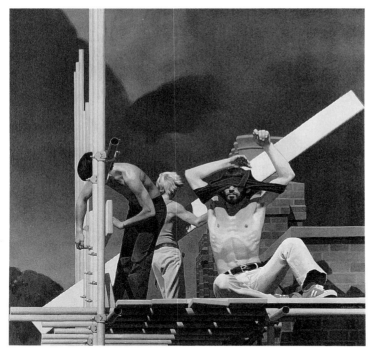

a

b

Anticipated Movement

Much of the implication of movement present in art is caused by our memory and past experience. We recognize temporary, unstable body positions and realize that change must be imminent. For example, we immediately "see" the action shown in **a.** The construction workers are in poses that we recognize as momentary, and we anticipate the change that is imminent. The worker at the right is taking off his shirt and obviously will not be in this position for more than a moment.

In a process called *kinesthetic empathy*, we tend to recreate unconsciously in our own bodies the actions we observe. We actually "feel" in our muscles the exertions of the athlete or dancer; we simultaneously stretch, push, or lean, though we are only watching. This involuntary reaction also applies to static images in art, where it can enhance the feeling of movement.

A feeling of movement can be heightened by contrast. Again, by memory, we realize that some things move and some do not. Thus, in **b** the figures seem to have more activity, more potential for movement, in their mobile positions because of the contrast with the large stolid building that appears so immobile. Our experience tells us that people move, but buildings rarely do.

Even nonobjective patterns can display movement through contrast. Because of past experience, we also see horizontal lines as quiet and inactive—just as our bodies are resting and still when we are lying horizontally. For a similar reason, we identify diagonal lines as suggestive of movement—just as our bodies lean and bend in such vigorous activities as sports. The horizontal emphasis of the building in **b** imparts a static feeling. But pure lines without subject reference can give the same result. A painting such as **c** seems dynamic and motion-filled. Here there are no recognizable objects, no forms that we can identify as being in fleeting positions. Yet we immediately sense not only the diagonal emphasis, but also the rapid, spontaneous strokes of the artist's brush in creating the painting. In a similar way, Mondrian's paintings with their constant repetition of careful, slowly rendered horizontal and vertical lines seem static and unmoving.

a Michael Leonard. *Scaffolders.* 1978. Acrylic on canvas, 41 × 40" (104 × 102 cm). Courtesy Fischer Fine Art Ltd., London.

b Nicholas Poussin. *The Rape of the Sabine Women.* Ca. 1636–1637. Oil on canvas, 5'1" × 6'10½" (1.55 × 2.1 m). Metropolitan Museum of Art, New York (Harris Brisbane Dick Fund).

c Michael Larionov. *Rayonist Composition: Domination of Red.* 1912–1913. Oil on canvas, 20¾ × 28½" (53 × 72 cm). Collection, The Museum of Modern Art, New York (gift of the artist).

c

a

b

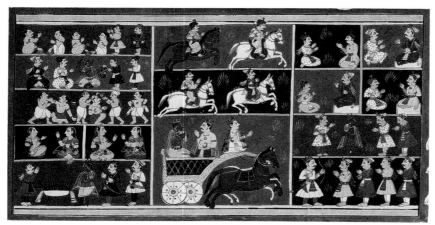

c

Ways to Suggest Motion

FIGURE REPEATED

Over the centuries, artists have devised various conventions to present an illusion of motion in art. One of the oldest devices is that of *repeating a figure*. As the thirteenth-century illumination in **a** illustrates, the figure of David from the Bible appears in different positions and situations. Architectural elements divide the format into four areas. In the upper left area, David with his slingshot meets the giant Goliath and prepares for battle. To the upper right David cuts off the slain giant's head as the Philistine soldiers leave. David presents the head to the King of Israel in the lower left vignette, and in the final scene David receives the gift of a cloak from an admirer.

This device was used widely in Oriental cultures as well as in Western medieval art. The figure of Krishna appears over and over in different positions and situations in the Indian miniature **(b).** It is interesting to note that this very old technique is still popular. The comic strips in our newspapers use exactly the same idea. In a series of boxes, we follow our favorite cartoon characters through a sequence of situations that relate a story.

Often the repeated figure, rather than being shown in a sequence of small pictures, merely reappears in one unified composition. This device occurred in Oriental art, was adopted in Western art, and remained popular as late as the Renaissance. Usually, a distinctive costume or color identified the repeated character, so that the repetition would be visually obvious. We see this in **c** a medieval wedding scene. During the festivities, a member of the wedding procession steps on the bride's train in the left foreground. In the right background, we recognize the same bride and groom figures, now retired alone to the nuptial chamber.

The effect can be quite subtle, as in *The Tribute Money* **(d),** painted about 1427. The tax collector demands the tribute money of Christ in the center, while Christ tells Peter to get the money from the fish's mouth. On the left, Peter kneels to get the money, and on the right he pays it to the tax collector. Without more than casual observation, however, we might miss the important sequential aspect.

a *David Slays Goliath and Cuts Off His Head.* Manuscript Illumination (M638 f 28v) from *Old Testament Miniatures,* Paris. Ca. 1245–1250. Tempera on vellum. Pierpont Morgan Library, New York.

b *Krishna Revealing His Nature as Vishnu.* Miniature from Malwa, India. Ca. 1730. Gouache or watercolor on paper, 8 × 14¾" (20 × 38 cm). Victoria and Albert Museum, London. Crown Copyright.

c *Betrothal of Reynaud de Mantauban and Clarisse, Daughter of King Yon of Gascogne.* Bibliotheque de l'Arsenal, Paris.

d Masaccio. *The Tribute Money.* Ca. 1427. Fresco, 8'4" × 19'8" (2.54 × 5.99 cm). Santa Maria del Carmine, Florence.

d

Ways to Suggest Motion

FUZZY OUTLINES

We readily interpret a photograph such as the one in **a** as a symbol of movement. With a fast shutter speed, moving images are frozen into "stop-action" photographs. Here the shutter speed is relatively slow, so that the sprinting commuter becomes a blurred, indistinct image that we read as an indication of the subject's movement. This is an everyday visual experience. When objects move through our field of vision quickly, we do not get a clear mental picture of them. A car will pass us on the highway so fast that we perceive only a colored blur. Details and edges of the form are lost in the rapidity of the movement.

The two figures in the drawing by the artist Daumier **(b)** suggest movement in this way. They are drawn with sketchy, incomplete, and overlapping lines to define their forms. The figure behind the rail literally wags his finger at the startled lawyer. The hand appears in rapid movement, for we get no one clear view in the blur of motion.

The painting in **c** gives us an extremely fuzzy and indistinct view of the foyer of the Paris Opera House. However, due to the lack of contour lines with no clear dividing edges, we get a very effective feeling of the crowd hurrying up the stairs to their seats in the loges and balcony. The scene does not imply movement by figures frozen in momentary postures, but tries to suggest that the action is taking place as we watch.

Even in purely nonobjective paintings, the blurred edge serves as an effective device. The vertical, sweeping shapes in **d** clearly suggest flowing and rapid movement.

a Elliott Erwitt. *Commuter.* 1964. Photograph.

b Honoré Daumier. *The Criminal Case.* N.d. Pen and ink and black chalk, 7⅛ × 11¼" (18 × 29 cm). Victoria and Albert Museum, London. Crown Copyright.

c Gaston La Touche. *The Staircase of the Paris Opera House.* 1905. Oil on panel, 14 × 13" (35.56 × 33 cm). Bury Street Gallery, London.

d Morris Louis. *Saraband.* 1959. Acrylic on canvas, 8'6" × 12'5" (2.57 × 3.78 m). Solomon R. Guggenheim Museum, New York.

a

b

c

d

a

b

c

Ways to Suggest Motion

MULTIPLE IMAGE

Another device for suggesting movement is called *multiple image*, illustrated in **a.** When we see one figure in an overlapping sequence of poses, the slight change in each successive position suggests movement taking place. Example **a** is an old photograph from the 1880s. The photographer, Thomas Eakins, was intrigued with the camera's capabilities for answering the visual problem of showing movement and analyzing it.

Example **b** shows this idea in a drawing by Ingres. While Ingres' motive was probably just to try two different positions for the figure, we get a clear suggestion of the figure moving in dance-like gestures.

Painters of the twentieth century have often been concerned with finding a visual language to express the increasingly dynamic quality of the world around us. Although at first glance very different, Duchamp's famous *Nude Descending a Staircase* **(c)** is actually much like the Eakins photograph **(a).** Again, multiple images of a figure are shown to suggest a body's movement in progress. Now the body forms are highly abstracted into simple geometric forms that repeat diagonally down the canvas as the nude "descends." Many curved lines (called *lines of force*) are added to show the pathway of movement. This is a device we commonly see, and immediately understand, in today's comic strips.

The play poster **(d)** uses the multiple image to suggest a very specific theme. Now the progressively altered image refers to the famous story where Dr. Jekyll changes into the monster, Mr. Hyde.

---

a Thomas Eakins. *Man Pole-Vaulting.* Ca. 1884. Metropolitan Museum of Art, New York (gift of Charles Brezler, 1941).

b Jean Auguste Dominique Ingres. *Female Nude.* Ca. 1826–1834. Pencil on white paper, 10⅞ × 11½" (27.8 × 29.6 cm). Musée Bonnat, Bayonne.

c Marcel Duchamp. *Nude Descending a Staircase, No. 2.* 1912. Oil on canvas, 4'10" × 2'11" (1.47 × 0.89 m). Philadelphia Museum of Art (Louise and Walter Arensberg Collection).

d *Dr. Jekyll and Mr. Hyde.* 1986. Poster for Seattle Children's Theatre, 18 × 24" (45.7 × 61 cm). Rick Eiber, Art Director; Rick Eiber, John Fortune, Designers; Rick Eiber Design, Seattle, WA.

d

12

C H A P T E R

VALUE

Introduction

Value is simply the artistic term for light and dark. An area's value is its relative lightness or darkness in a given context. Only through changes of light and dark can we perceive anything. Light reveals forms; in a dark room at night we *see* nothing and bump into furniture and walls. The page you are reading now is legible only because the darkness of the type contrasts with the whiteness of the background paper. Even the person (or animal) who is physiologically unable to perceive color can function with only minimal difficulties by perception based on varying tones of gray.

Example **a** is a scale of seven values of gray. These are termed *achromatic* grays, as they are mixtures of only black and white: No color (or chroma) is used.

The term *value-contrast* refers to the relationship between areas of dark and light. Because the scale in **a** is arranged in sequential order, the contrast between any two adjoining areas is rather slight and termed *low-value* contrast. The center gray circles are all the same middle value. It is interesting to note how this consistent center gray seems to change visually depending on the background. Indeed, it is hard to believe that the circles on the far left and far right are precisely the same value.

The scale in **a** shows only seven basic steps. Theoretically between black and white there could be an almost unlimited number of steps. Studies have shown that the average eye can discern somewhere around forty variations in value. The artist may use as many or as few values as his artistic purposes indicate, though at times the nature of the chosen medium may influence the result. The drawing of the cat in **b** uses a very broad range of values. The artist, Charles Sheeler, drawing with a conté crayon, skillfully exploited the medium's softness to create many grays and an interesting design of dark and light contrasts.

Value and color are related. Color, based on wave-lengths of light, offers a much broader field of visual differences and contrasts. But grayed neutrals (now called *chromatic* grays) can also be produced by mixing certain colors, which result in different tones than those in **a**. A further relationship of value and color is that every color is, in itself, also simultaneously a certain value. Pure yellow is a light (high-value) color corresponding to a very light gray in terms of light reflection. Purple is basically a dark, low-value color that would match a very dark gray.

The painting in **c** is an illustration of a work done in color but here reproduced just in the corresponding tones of gray. There is not as much contrast of dark and light as in **b**. The artist depended more on sheer color changes—lively, unexpected colors with unusual combinations of hues—all of which we cannot appreciate in this reproduction. Obviously, we miss much of this work's visual pleasure. Yet the basic structure is still clear; we can still "read" the subject matter and understand the various shapes. The reproduction in **c** presents what is called the *value pattern* of the original painting.

a A value scale of gray. The center circles are identical in value.

b Charles Sheeler. *Feline Felicity.* 1934. Black conté crayon on white paper, 21¾ × 17⅞″ (56 × 46 cm). Fogg Art Museum, Harvard University, Cambridge, MA (Louise E. Bettens Fund).

c Franz Marc. *The Yellow Cow.* 1911. Oil on canvas, 4′7⅜″ × 6′2½″ (1.41 × 1.89 m). Solomon R. Guggenheim Museum, New York.

a

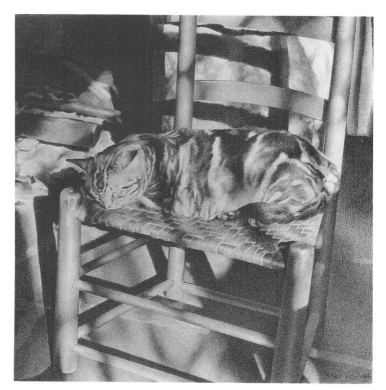

b

c

a

b

c

Value Pattern

In describing paintings or designs, we often speak of their *value pattern*. This term refers to the arrangement and the amount of variation in light and dark, independent of the colors used.

When value contrast is minimized and all the values are within a limited range with only small variation, the result is a restrained, subtle effect. The impression is one of understatement, whether the value range is limited to lights (*high* key is a term often used) or darks (*low* key). In Richard Dadd's watercolor **(a),** the values are all extremely light, with really no contrasting dark areas, just a few slightly darker lines here and there. The painting in **b** shows the opposite approach, an extreme contrast of dark and light. This is a Baroque painting, done in a period when artists purposely accentuated value contrasts to portray exciting themes. The violent and gory subject of Artemisia Gentileschi's painting **(b)** receives an aptly emotional visual treatment. The light from the single candle casts dramatic, sudden shadows throughout the scene, achieving almost a theatrical effect.

Our different responses to **a** and **b** illustrate how value alone can create an immediate emotional reaction. The artist can choose a value pattern to elicit emotional reactions in the viewer. Closely related values are calm and quiet. The theme of the harem in **a** is shown with unnaturally light values, and the shapes are barely discernible. An exotic, mystical, almost magical mood results. On the other hand, sharp value contrasts suggest drama, excitement, even conflict. Certainly, the gruesome theme of **b** would not be communicated by the limited range of values in **a**. An entirely different mood would have been presented.

In the same way, overall darkness may provide feelings of sadness, depression, and even mystery. Lighter values, being brighter, seem less serious or threatening. Specific colors will always evoke emotional reactions, but the value pattern alone can be important in expressing a theme.

The painting in **b** shows values that could be seen in a dark room lit by a single candle. The painting in **c** does not refer to any specific light source but also involves an extreme contrast of light and dark. The artist here has deliberately exaggerated (or "heightened") the value contrast. The shapes have been simplified into a pattern of mostly black and white with only a few gray areas. This produces an unusual and highly dramatic image of what could have seemed a rather ordinary scene if done with a naturalistic value pattern.

---

a Richard Dadd. *Fantasie de l'Harem Égyptien.* 1865. Watercolor, 10⅞ × 7" (48 × 18 cm). Ashmolean Museum, Oxford.

b Artemesia Gentileschi. *Judith and Maidservant with the Head of Holofernes.* Ca. 1625. Oil on canvas, 6'½" × 4'7¾" (1.84 × 1.42 m). © The Detroit Institute of Arts (gift of Leslie H. Green).

c Robert Harvey. *Brother Home on Leave.* 1964. Oil on canvas, 48 × 48" (121.9 × 121.9 cm). Mead Art Collection, Dayton, OH.

Value as Emphasis

A valuable use of dark-and-light contrast is to create a focal point or center of attention in a design. A visual emphasis or "starting point" is often desired. A thematically important character or feature can be visually emphasized by value contrast. High dark-and-light contrast instantly attracts our attention. By planning high contrast in one area and subdued contrast elsewhere, the artist can be assured where the viewer's eye will be directed first.

The focal point in Gustave Moreau's painting **(a)** is immediately established by value. Almost the entire painting is done in closely related, very dark values. The dancing figure of Salome is then accentuated by her sudden, much lighter value. She appears almost as if in a spotlight on a darkened stage.

Moreau's use of value is very effective, if not overly subtle. The painting by Hopper **(b)** uses the same technique in a less obvious way. The sharp white of the interior of the brightly lit cafe contrasts with the general darkness outside. This light then "frames" the several dark figures, who become the focal point of the painting. The general isolation of these dark spots reinforces the quiet, almost melancholy mood of the painting.

Paintings **a** and **b** are, of course, done in color. But the black-and-white reproductions here are valuable to show the artists' reliance on value contrast, irrespective of the particular colors involved. Most artists are as aware of the value pattern they create as of the pattern of various colors. The artistic choice is often not green or red but how dark (or light) a green or red to use.

When value contrast is evenly distributed throughout a design, the result is usually a work with overall emphasis and no clear visual importance of any one part. This is sometimes a conscious choice of the artist, but somewhat rare. The early Cubist painters stressed value rather than color differences, often with quite limited contrast in their patterns of innumerable planes. The values in the Picasso portrait **(c)** are closely related, but the very slightly higher contrast around the head does establish a focal point.

a Gustave Moreau. *Salome Dancing Before Herod.* 1876. Oil on canvas, 36½ × 24″ (93 × 61 cm). Musée Gustave Moreau, Paris.

b Edward Hopper. *Nighthawks.* 1942. Oil on canvas, 2′6″ × 5′ (0.76 × 1.44 m). © 1989 The Art Institute of Chicago. All rights reserved.

c Pablo Picasso. *Daniel-Henry Kahnweiler.* 1910. Oil on canvas, 39⅝ × 28⅝″ (101 × 73 cm). © 1989 The Art Institute of Chicago (gift of Mrs. Gilbert W. Chapman in memory of Charles B. Goodspeed). All rights reserved.

a

c

b

a

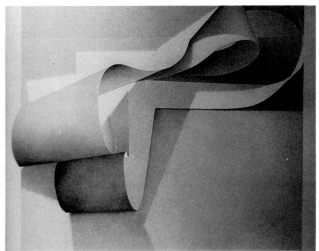

b

c

d

Value and Space

One of the most important uses of gradations of dark and light is to suggest volume or space.

On a flat surface, value can be used to impart a three-dimensional quality to shapes. During the Renaissance, the word *chiaroscuro* was coined to describe the artistic device of using light and dark to imply depth and volume in a painting or drawing. *Chiaroscuro* is a combination of the Italian words for "light" and "dark." A drawing using only line is very effective in showing shapes. By varying the weight of the line, an artist may imply dimension or solidity, but the effect is subtle. When areas of dark and light are added, we begin to feel the three-dimensional quality of forms. This is apparent in *Portrait of a Man* **(a).** Here the head has been shaded with values that give it a feeling of volume and roundness, especially in comparison with the body, which is rendered merely in line.

The drawing in **b** shows the effective feeling of three-dimensional depth and volume that shading can suggest on a flat surface. As all photographers soon learn, the light direction is important: Front lighting flattens form; side lighting emphasizes volume; back or below lighting can distort form into unexpected patterns **(c)** used for design or emotional reasons.

Along the same idea, another aspect of value's ability to suggest depth is important. Much art has been, and is, concerned with producing a simulation of our three-dimensional world. On a two-dimensional piece of paper or canvas, an *illusion* of space is desired—and perhaps not just the roundness of a head, but a whole scene receding far into the distance. Here again the use of value can be a valuable tool of the artist. High-value contrast seems to come forward, to be actually *closer,* whereas areas of lesser contrast recede or stay back, suggesting distance. Notice how effectively Caspar Friedrich has used this technique in painting **d.** The figure on the rocks in front is sharply dark against the rest of the picture. Then each receding rock, wave, and bit of land becomes progressively lighter and closer to the value of the sky. An illusion of great depth is thus created by manipulating the various values.

This technique does reproduce what our eyes see: Far-off images visually become grayer and less distinct as the distance increases. In art, this is called *aerial,* or *atmospheric, perspective.*

a Rico Lebrun. *Portrait of a Man.* 1939. Ink and chalk. Private collection.
b Sue Hettmansperger. *Untitled.* 1975. Watercolor and pencil, 23 × 25″ (58 × 64 cm). North Carolina National Bank.
c Alfred Leslie. *Alfred Leslie.* 1974. Lithograph, 40 × 30″ (102 × 76 cm). Publisher Landfall Press, Inc., Chicago.
d Caspar David Friedrich. *The Wanderer Above the Sea of Mist.* Ca. 1817–1818. Oil on canvas, 38⅜ × 29¼″ (99 × 75 cm). Kunsthalle, Hamburg.

a

b

c

d

e

Techniques

The use of value in a work of art is what we would commonly call *shading*. However, to say that an artist uses shading does little to describe the final work, as there are so many techniques and hence many visual effects available. Artistic aims vary, of course, from producing a naturalistic rendition of some visual image to a completely nonobjective work that uses dark and light simply as an element to provide added visual interest to the design. Even with a similar purpose, however, the same subject done by the same artist will be very different depending on the chosen medium and technique. These examples can show you just a few of the almost unlimited possibilities.

Pencil, charcoal, chalk, and conté crayon are very familiar media to art students. Being soft media, they are capable of providing (if desired) very gradual changes of dark to light. The Prud'hon drawing **(a)** shows the subtle and gradual transitions possible.

A medium such as black ink, by its nature, gives decidedly sharp value contrast. But this can be altered in several ways. The artist may use what is called *cross-hatching* (black lines of various densities that, seen against the white background, can give the impression of different grays). Again, variations are possible. These lines may be done with careful, repetitive precision (as seen in many drawings and etchings) or in a loose, freely spontaneous manner **(b).** An artist may also choose the technique of *wash drawing*, in which the black ink is mixed with water, diluting the ink to produce desired shades of gray.

There are other possibilities. The Van Gogh drawing **(c)** creates areas of gray by means of small strokes of the pen—sometimes small, repeated lines and sometimes dots. The use of dots to create visual grays is a very common procedure, though we may not realize it. All of the black-and-white *half-tones* we see daily in newspapers, books, and magazines are actually areas of tiny black dots in various concentrations to produce visual grays. This is a photo-mechanical process, but the same effect can be seen in Seurat's drawing **(d).** Here, the "dots" are created by the artist scraping a soft conté crayon over a heavily textured white paper. Again, dots of black produce visual grays.

Along the same idea **e** presents a definite visual feeling of grays and, hence, dimension and volume. But this is a "drawing" done by a computer. The grays are actually created by the positioning of hundreds of tiny computer symbols of various densities that combine with the white background to give us the impression of many different grays.

---

a Pierre Paul Prud'hon. *La Source.* Ca. 1801. Black and white chalk on blue-gray paper, 21³/₁₆ × 15⁵/₁₆″ (54 × 39 cm). Sterling and Francine Clark Art Institute, Williamstown, MA.

b Henri Matisse. *Nude in Armchair.* Ca. 1906. India ink with brush, 25⁷/₈ × 18³/₈″ (65.8 × 46.6 cm). © 1989 The Art Institute of Chicago (gift of Mrs. Potter Palmer). All rights reserved.

c Vincent Van Gogh. *La Crau as Seen From Montmajour.* 1888. Black chalk, pen, reed pen and brown and black ink, 19¼ × 24″ (49 × 61 cm). Foundation Vincent Van Gogh. National Museum Vincent Van Gogh, Amsterdam.

d Georges Seurat. *Seated Boy With Straw Hat.* (Study for *The Bathers*). 1882. Conte crayon, 9½ × 12¼″ (24.13 × 31.1 cm). Yale University Art Gallery, New Haven (Everett V. Meeks Fund).

e Leon Harmon and Kenneth Knowlton. *Nude (Study in Perception).* 1966. Computerized, alphanumeric print, 30 × 144″ (76.2 × 365.8 cm). Courtesy AT&T Bell Laboratories.

13

C H A P T E R

COLOR

Introduction

It is not only the professional artist or designer who deals with color. All of us make color decisions almost every day. We constantly choose items to purchase of which the color is a major factor. Our world today is marked by bold uses of color in every area of ordinary living. We can make color choices for everything from home appliances to bank checks—it seems that most things we use have blossomed out in bright colors. Fashion design, interior design, architecture, industrial design—all fields in art are now increasingly concerned with color.

So, everyone can profit by knowing some basic color principles. Unfortunately, the study of color can be rather complex. The word *color* has so many aspects that it means different things to a physicist, optician, psychiatrist, poet, lighting engineer, and painter, and the analysis of color becomes a multifaceted report in which many experts competently describe their findings. Shelves of books in the library on the topic attest that a comprehensive study of color from all viewpoints is impossible in limited space.

However, any study of color must start with a few important, basic facts. The essential fact of color theory is that color is a property of *light,* not an object itself. This property of light was illustrated by Sir Isaac Newton in the seventeenth century, when he put white light through a prism **(a).** The prism broke up white light into the familiar rainbow of hues. Objects have no color of their own but merely the ability to reflect certain rays of white light, which contain all the colors. Blue objects *absorb* all the rays except the blue ones, and these are *reflected* to our eyes. Black objects *absorb* all the rays; white objects *reflect* all of them. The significance of this fact for the artist is that as light changes, color will change.

But although color indeed comes from light,

the guidelines of color mixing and usage are different depending on whether the color source is light or pigments and dyes. Rays of light are direct light, whereas the color of paint is reflected light. Color from light combines and forms new visual sensations based on what is called the *additive* system. On the other hand, pigments combine in the *subtractive* system. This term is appropriate. Blue paint is "blue" because when light hits its surface the pigment absorbs (or "subtracts") all of the color components except the blue that is reflected to our eyes. Artists should be aware of both systems. The painter, of course, will be mainly concerned with the subtractive, whereas the stage lighting designer, photographer, and often the interior designer will be concerned with the additive.

Lights projected from *different* sources mix according to the additive method. The diagram in **b** shows the three primary colors of light—red, green, and blue—and the colors produced where two hues overlap. The three primaries combined will produce white light. *Complementary* (or opposite) hues in light (red/cyan, blue/yellow, green/magenta) when mixed will again produce an achromatic grey or white. Where light from a cyan (blue-green) spotlight and from a red spotlight overlap, the visual sensation is basically colorless. Combining these two colors in pigment would produce a neutral "mud"—anything but white.

Recognize that these combinations of light are from *separate* sources. Placing a yellow and blue filter on the *same* spotlight will result in a green light, now functioning according to the subtractive system.

Because this book aims primarily at use in studio art classes, where the usual medium is paint, the information in this section refers mainly to the subtractive system of color usage.

---

a A ray of white light projected through a prism separates into the hues seen in a rainbow.

b Colors of light mix according to the additive process.

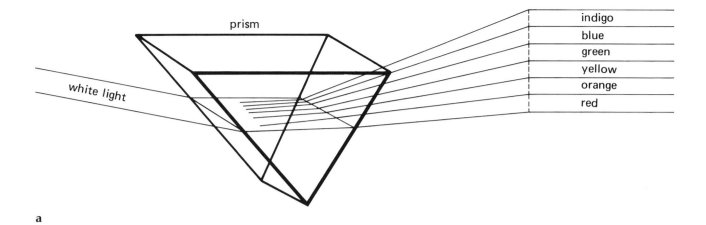

prism

white light

indigo
blue
green
yellow
orange
red

a

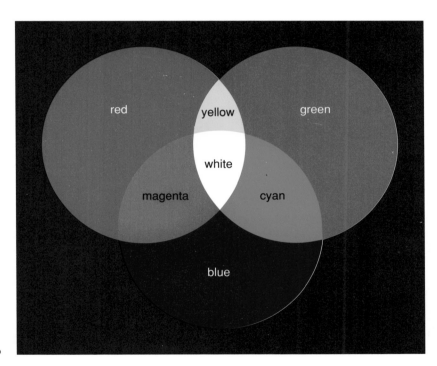

red   yellow   green

white

magenta   cyan

blue

b

a

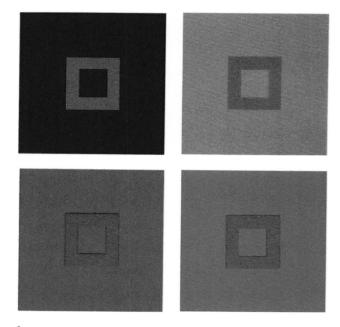

b

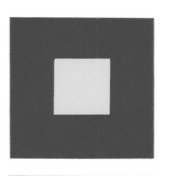

c

Color Characteristics

Color theory is an extremely complex science. A thorough study of such factors as the various light wavelengths of different colors or the color/heat relationship is interesting but complicated and goes beyond our concern here.

Color has a basic, instinctive, visual appeal. Great art has been created in black and white, but few artists have totally ignored the added visual interest that color lends. The uninhibited use of color has been a primary characteristic of art in this century. Some artists use color primarily as an emotional element, and many artists use color in a strictly intuitive way. However, there have been artists who studied color per se and thereby have added immeasurably to our knowledge of color and color usage. Today's artists and students (and authors) owe a great debt to the contemporary American artist Josef Albers, who as painter and teacher has devoted a career to the study of color and color relationships. His books and paintings have contributed invaluably to our knowledge of color. Many of the concepts in this discussion are reflections of his research and teaching.

Color is a product of light. Therefore as light changes, all color references will change. What color is grass? Green? Grass may be almost gray at dawn, bright green at noon, and nearly black at midnight. There is no one consistent color for any thing or object. Though this is simple visual fact, many of us have been rather unaware of this phenomenon, and many artists have heightened our perception. With a merely casual glance at Monet's painting (a) we could dismiss the color usage as whim or personal license. However, a careful look at a similar sunset scene would show the artist's color use as highly descriptive of a fleeting moment.

Related to this same idea, one other color phenomenon is important: Colors change according to their surroundings. Even in the same light, a color will appear different depending on the colors that are adjacent to it. Rarely do we see a color by itself. Perhaps an occasional room or a certain stage set presents just one color, but this is unusual. Normally, colors are seen in conjunction with others, and the visual differences are often amazing. A change in value (dark and light) is a common occurrence. Example **b** illustrates that even the color effect itself changes. The smaller red-purple squares are identical; the visual differences are caused by the various background colors these squares are placed against.

The phenomenon of color change is another variable. In working with color, you will soon discover that some colors are more susceptible to change than others. In looking at **b**, it is hard to believe the four pink squares are the identical color. In **c**, however, the two yellow areas, despite different backgrounds, still look about the same. With pure, vibrant colors, optical changes will be very slight. Grayed, neutral colors (called *broken* colors) are constantly changing in different contexts.

---

a Claude Monet. *Poplars on the Bank of the Epte River.* 1891. Oil on canvas, 39½ × 25¾" (100 × 65 cm). Philadelphia Museum of Art (bequest of Anne Thomson as a memorial to her father, Frank Thomson and her mother, Mary Elizabeth Clarke Thomson).
b The red-purple squares, although seemingly different, are identical.
c A brilliant, vibrant color will not show much change despite different surroundings.

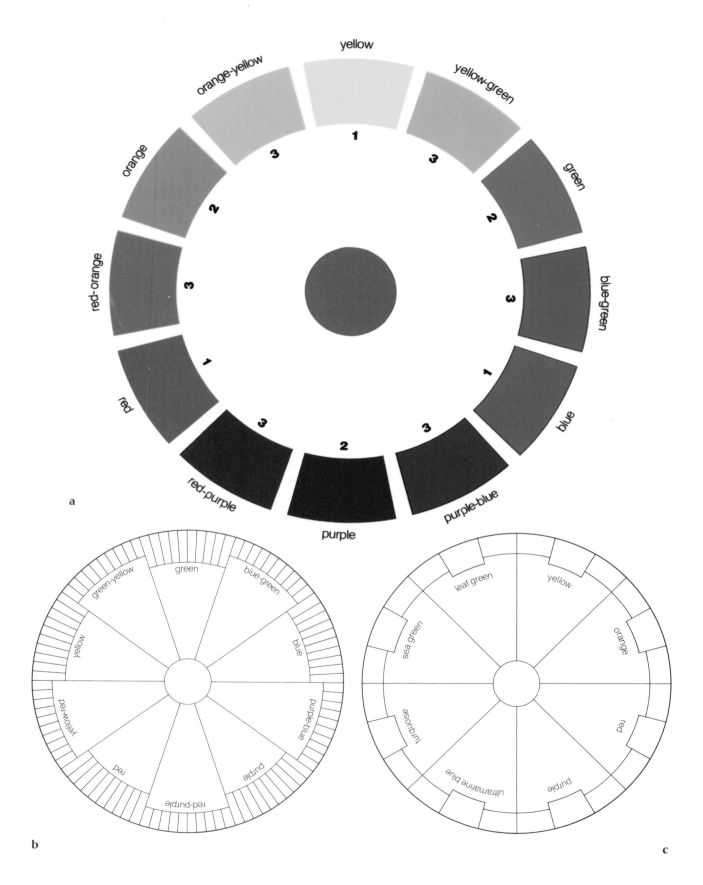

yellow

orange-yellow

yellow-green

orange

green

3

1

3

2

2

red-orange

3

3

blue-green

3

1

red

blue

3

3

2

3

red-purple

purple-blue

purple

a

green-yellow

green

blue-green

yellow

blue

yellow-red

purple-blue

red

purple

red-purple

b

leaf green

yellow

sea green

orange

turquoise

red

ultramarine blue

purple

c

Properties of Color

HUE

The first property of color is what we call *hue*. Hue simply refers to the name of the color. Red, orange, green, and purple are hues. Although the words *hue* and *color* are often used as synonyms, this is a bit confusing, as there is a distinction between the two terms. The word *hue* describes the visual sensation of the different parts of the color spectrum. However, one hue can be varied to produce many colors. So even though there are relatively few hues, there can be an almost unlimited number of colors. Pink, rose, scarlet, maroon, and crimson are all colors, but the hue in each case is red. We are all aware that in the world of commercial products, color names abound; Plum, Adobe, Colonial Blue, Desert Sunset, Mayan Gold, and Avocado are a few examples. These often romantic images are extremely inexact terms that mean only what the manufacturers think they mean. The same hue (or color) can have dozens of different commercial names.

Example **a** shows what is called a *color wheel*, the most common organization of the basic colors. The wheel system dates back to the early eighteenth century. This particular organization uses twelve hues, which are divided into three categories.

The three *primary* (1) colors are red, yellow, and blue. From these, all other colors are mixed.

The three *secondary* (2) colors are mixtures of the two primaries: Red and yellow make orange, yellow and blue make green, blue and red make purple. Because of the relative strength of the various hues, a visual middle secondary does not always contain *equal* amounts of the two colors.

The six *tertiary* (3) colors are mixtures of a primary and an adjacent secondary: Blue and green make blue-green, red and purple make red-purple and so on.

The color wheel of twelve hues is purely arbitrary, as is the choice of primary colors. Two other color systems are shown for comparison. Example **b** diagrams the Munsell color organization, **c** the Ostwald wheel. Both of these cite different primary colors. The Munsell system involves the five primaries shown, with five "intermediates" (red plus yellow does not produce "orange," but the intermediate "yellow-red") and a complete wheel of 100 hues. The Ostwald wheel is based on four primaries, with a total of twenty-four hues on the complete wheel. All these color organizations are satisfactory, although one or another might be preferred for a specific color problem. This book will use the basic twelve-color wheel because it works perfectly well for most design problems involving the usual pigment or dye.

a Color wheel showing primary, secondary, and tertiary colors.
b The Munsell Color System.
c The Ostwald Color System.

Properties of Color

VALUE

The second property of color is *value,* which refers to the lightness or darkness of the hue. Example **a** shows a value scale of blue. Only one hue is present, but the blue varies widely in light and dark. In pigment, value can be altered by adding white or black paint to the color. Adding white lightens the color and produces a *tint,* or high-value color. Adding black darkens the color and produces a *shade,* or low-value color. Individual perception varies, but most people can distinguish at least forty tints and shades of any color.

Not all the colors on the color wheel are shown at the same value. Each is shown at *normal* value, with the pure color unmixed and undiluted. The normal values of yellow and of blue, for example, are radically different. Because yellow is a light, or high-value, color, a yellow value scale would show many more shades than tints. The blue scale **(a)** shows more tints, because normal blue is darker than middle value.

Value, like color itself, is variable and entirely dependent on surrounding hues for its visual sensation. In example **a** a value scale of seven blues from dark to light, the center circle in each area is a constant middle-value blue, but its value appears to change depending on the square in which it is placed. The center circle seems much darker on the lighter blues than on the darker ones. In **b** the center green area appears much lighter and more luminous on the black background than on the white.

Colors changed by their context is a well-known occurrence. Many authors have termed this the *spreading effect,* where the color sensation "spreads" to affect the adjacent hues. Often artists have outlined their colored areas with black line. It has been observed that this technique does make the enclosed color seem visually richer and clearer in tone. The dark separating form seems to inhibit the spreading effect and lets each color display its characteristic sensation independently.

In stained glass, the dark black leading around the colored glass segments is a structural necessity to hold the pieces in place. The unusual color brilliance of the Byzantine mosaics has been attributed to the slight dark lines that enclose each brightly colored tile. Outlining colored forms with dark lines is common to many periods of art and many media, as the sixth-century Peruvian weaving **(c)** demonstrates. In eras when a naturalistic, purely visual image was desired, outlining was condemned as unrealistic and "primitive," but it has served as a valuable artistic device to enhance color over the centuries, including twentieth-century art.

Incidentally, an outline in white or a light-value color **(d)** achieves the opposite effect. The enclosed color now seems less rich, less dynamic, and jewellike. The white apparently "spreads" to lend a slightly washed-out or tinted effect to the outlined hue.

SEE ALSO: VALUE TECHNIQUES, PAGE 223.

a The blue scale shows variations from dark to light. The circles in the centers are all middle value, although they seem different against lighter or darker backgrounds.

b The same color will appear to change in value, depending upon the surrounding color.

c Wine-red veil in Nazca style. From southern Peru. 400–600 A.D. Woven llama wool, 38⅛ × 74¾" (97 × 190 cm). Staatliches Museum für Völkerkunde, Munich (Collection Heinrich Hardt).

d Guillaume Beverloo Corneille. *Discovery of the Island.* 1965. Oil on canvas, 31⅝ × 25⅜" (80 × 64 cm). Private collection.

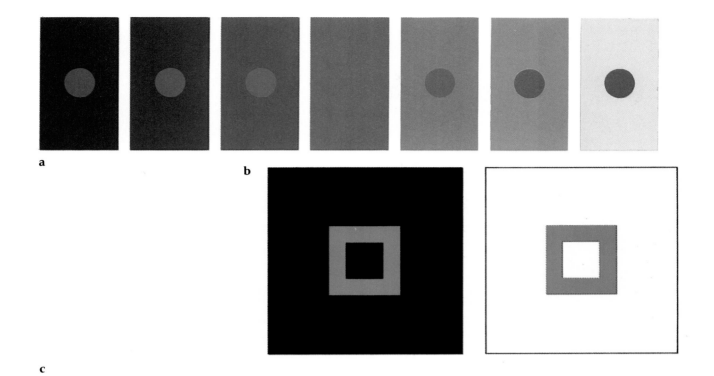

a

b

c

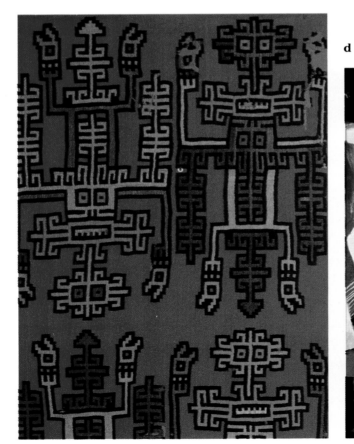

d

a

b

c

d

Properties of Color

INTENSITY/COMPLEMENTARY COLORS

The third property of color is *intensity*, which refers to the brightness of a color. Because a color is at full intensity only when pure and unmixed, a relationship exists between *value* and *intensity*. Mixing black or white with a color changes its value but at the same time affects its intensity. To see the distinction between the two terms, look at the two tints (high value) of red in example **a.** The tints have about the same degree of lightness, yet one might be called ''rose,'' the other ''shocking pink.'' The two colors are very different in their visual effect, and the difference comes from brightness or intensity. Intensity is sometimes called *chroma,* or *saturation.*

There are two ways to lower the intensity of a color, to make a color less bright, more neutral, and duller. One way is to mix gray with the color. Depending on the gray used, you can dull a color without changing its value. The second way is to mix a color with its *complement,* the color directly across from it on the color wheel. Example **b** shows an intensity scale involving the complementary colors blue and orange. Neutralized (low-intensity) versions of a color are often called *tones.* In **b** we see three tones of blue and three tones of orange. As progressively more orange is added to the blue, the blue becomes duller, more grayed. The same is true of the orange, which becomes browner when blue is added. When complements are mixed in equal amounts, they cancel each other out, and a muddy neutral tone results.

Complementary colors are direct opposites in position and in character. Mixing complementary colors together dulls them, but when complementary colors are placed *next to each other,* they intensify each other's brightness. When blue and orange are side by side, each color will appear brighter than in any other context. This effect is called *simultaneous contrast,* meaning that each complement simultaneously intensifies the visual brilliance of the other, so that the colors appear to vibrate. Artists use this visual effect when they wish to produce brilliant color. The Art Nouveau Tapestry in **c** employs complementary colors. Here the weirdly flowing red shapes of the angels' dresses contrast with the flat areas of grass in complementary green. The small round purple shapes of the far background trees stand out vividly against the complementary yellow sky.

The colors of Richard Lytle's painting **(d)** are based on the complementary red and green. It can be seen here that many of the colors are indeed of low saturation. But even so, the basic color contrast (plus value changes) produces a very dramatic image. The forms suggestive of plant life extend and entwine across the canvas, often changing color quite abruptly, along vertical divisions. There is an ambivalent spatial quality as forms recede and then change color and come forward.

Another peculiar visual phenomenon of complementary colors is called *afterimage.* Stare at an area of intense color for a minute or so, and then glance away at a white piece of paper or wall. Suddenly, an area of the complementary color will seem to appear. For example, when you look at the white wall after staring at a red shape, a definite green area in somewhat the same shape will seem to take form on the wall.

---

a Two tints of red at the same value have different intensities.

b One way to lower the intensity of a color is to mix it with its complement.

c Henry van de Velde. *Engelwache (Angel Vigil).* 1893. Tapestry, 4'6⅜'' × 7'6⅞'' (1.4 × 2.33 m). Museum Bellerive, Zurich.

d Richard Lytle. *Early Sound Cantabria.* 1972. Oil on canvas, 7' × 7'6'' (2.1 × 2.3 m). Collection of the artist.

Visual Color Mixing

The mixing of pigments combines along certain guidelines to create new colors. However, muddy or dull colors are often the result. Mixing blue paint and red paint does produce a purple of sorts, though it is usually quite brownish and neutral. The mixture is not the color sensation we think of in our minds as "purple"—the purple in the robes of kings or the iris in the garden.

Unhappily, even chemically created purple paints cannot truly re-create the visual quality of some summer evening's sunset sky. Pigment simply will never reproduce the luminous and brilliant quality of light. Recognizing this, artists have struggled with the problem and tried various techniques to overcome it. One attempt is what is called *visual mixing*. Rather than *mixing* two colors on the palette, artists place two pure colors side by side in small areas so the viewer's eye (at a certain distance) will do the mixing. Or perhaps they drag a brush of thick pigment of one color loosely across a field of another color. The uneven paint application allows bits and pieces of the background to show through. Again the pure colors are mixed in our perception, not on the canvas.

Visual mixing was highly systematized in such a movement as *Pointillism* in the nineteenth century. As the name implies, "points" or small dots of various colors were juxtaposed to produce different color sensations. Though many artists experimented in this area, it is the French artist Georges Seurat that we immediately associate with the idea **(a).** A related movement was called *Divisionism,* which used the same basic idea, though perhaps with fine lines rather than dots.

Precisely how successful these artists were in their attempts to create color brilliance depends on which expert or critic you read. However, the basic idea of visual mixing is used in many areas. In creating mosaics, stirring up a bowl of red and blue tiles will not, of course, produce purple tesserae. Instead, small pieces of pure-colored tiles are interspersed to produce the effect of many other intermediate colors. The same process is employed in creating tapestries. Weavers working with a limited number of colored yarns or threads can intermingle them, so that at a distance the eye merges them and creates an impression of many hues and values **(b).** A more everyday example is plaid or tartan fabric. From a distance, the material can seem to be a pattern of many colors and values. On close inspection probably just two or three colored threads have been woven in various densities to produce all the visual variations.

A version of the pointillist technique is now used everyday in a photomechanical adaptation in the printing of color pictures. The numerous colors we see in printed reproductions are all produced by usually just four basic colors in a small dot pattern. The dots in this case are so tiny that we are totally unaware of them unless we use a magnifying glass to visually enlarge them **(c).**

---

a Georges Seurat. *Bathers, Asnières.* 1883–1884. Oil on canvas, 79⅛ × 118⅛" (201 × 300 cm). National Gallery, London. Reproduced by courtesy of the Trustees.

b Workshop of Nicolas Bataille. *Arthur with Three Cardinals,* detail from the *Nine Heroes* series. Ca. 1385. Tapestry, 11'6½" × 10' (3.51 × 3.05 m). Metropolitan Museum of Art, New York (Cloisters Collection, Munsey Fund, 1932).

c Photograph with enlarged photomechanical dot pattern shows blending into different colors.

a

b

c

a

b

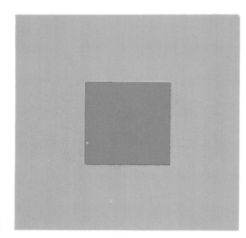

c

d

Cool/Warm Colors

Cool colors? *Warm* colors? These may seem odd adjectives to apply to the visual sensation of color, as ''cool'' and ''warm'' are sensations of touch, not sight. Nevertheless, we are all familiar with the terms and continually refer to colors this way. Because of the learned association of color and objects, we continue to identify and relate the sensations of the different senses. Hence, red and orange (fire) and yellow (sunlight) become identified as warm colors. Similarly, blue (sky, water) and green (grass, plants) are always thought of as cool colors.

Touching an area of red will assuredly not burn your hand, but *looking* at red will indeed induce a feeling of warmth. The effect may be purely psychological, but the results are very real. We have all read of the workers in an office painted blue complaining of the chill and actually getting colds. The problem was solved not by raising the thermostat but by repainting the office in warm tones of brown. The painting by Childe Hassam in **a** makes us truly feel the cool, misty atmosphere of the foggy straits of San Francisco Bay by his emphasis on the blue side of the spectrum.

On the color wheel, the tertiary red-orange appears as the warmest color, and the opposite blue-green seems the coldest of the hues. We generally think of the colors yellow through red-violet as the warm side of the color wheel and yellow-green through violet as the cool segment. The visual effects are quite variable, however, and again depend a great deal on the context in which we see the color. In **b** the green square appears very warm surrounded by a background of blue. But in **c** the identical green, when placed on an orange background, shifts and becomes a cooler tone.

As warm colors tend to advance, while cool colors seem to recede, the artist may use the warm/cool relationship to establish a feeling of depth and volume. Probably no group of artists have investigated and expanded our ideas of color more than the Impressionists. The blue and purple shadows (instead of gray and black) that so shocked the nineteenth-century public seem to us today perfectly logical and reasonable. In Renoir's still life **(d),** *Fruits of the Midi,* notice how the rounded volumes are molded by the artist's use of warm and cool contrasts. The highlights in warm tones gradually change to cooler colors expressing the shadow areas.

a Childe Hassam. *The Silver Veil and the Golden Gate.* 1914. Oil on canvas, 29⅝ × 31⅝" (75 × 80 cm). Valparaiso University Art Galleries and Collections, Valparaiso, Indiana (Sloan Collection. Sloan Fund Purchase).
b A colored area on a cool background will appear warmer in tone.
c The same color surrounded by a warm background seems cool.
d Auguste Renoir. *Fruits of the Midi.* 1881. Oil on canvas, 20 × 27" (50.7 × 65.3 cm). © 1989 The Art Institute of Chicago (Mr. and Mrs. Martin A. Ryerson Collection). All rights reserved.

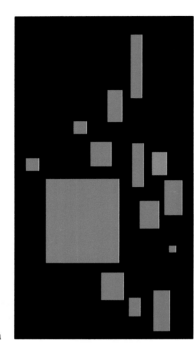
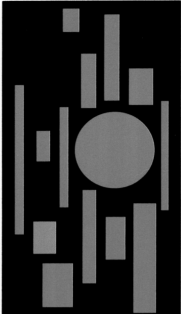

a

b

c

Color as Emphasis

Areas of emphasis in a work of art create visual interest and, naturally, have been carefully planned by the artist. Color is very often the means chosen to provide this emphasis—color is probably the most direct device to use. When planning emphasis, we might think of using a larger size somewhere, or perhaps a change in shape, or isolating one element by itself. As can be seen by the diagrams in **a,** the use of color will dominate over these other devices. You will notice that the accented color is not a radically different hue or very different in value or intensity. Such contrasts, of course, would heighten the effect. But **a** shows that color by its very character commands attention.

Sometimes the artist may wish to create a definite focal point or center of attention that the observer will see first. A bright or vivid color, such as the slanted V-shape in Franz Kline's painting **(b),** immediately will attract our eye. The bold color and spontaneous brush stroke establish the feeling of dynamic excitement characteristic of the whole work. The yellow shape is not the only area of yellow in the painting, but it is emphasized by being surrounded by the dark blue-blacks. The color value contrast is also important here.

In Winslow Homer's painting **(c)** bright yellow and red are used to emphasize the central figure preparing his carnival costume. The painting has dramatic contrasts of light and shadow throughout, but the vivid color notes bring our eye to the focal point.

The term *emphasis* can describe different visual effects. Perhaps the term is used to denote the creation of a strong, definite focal point such as seen in **b** and **c.** However, emphasis can apply also to the placement of quite subtle color *accents* within a composition. The painting by Caillebotte **(d)** is an example. Various tones of cold blues and grays dominate the picture, with sharp white contrasts in the snow-covered roofs. However, amid this cold, snowy scene also are found a few subtle accents of warm brownish-red on several chimneys and on a building in the center background. These red areas are neither brilliant in color nor eye-demanding as focal points. They are simply contrasting accents. A simple *change* in color, with the introduction of a contrasting color, was enough to provide the truly quiet visual emphasis.

---

a Color is so strong a visual element that it will dominate other devices to establish emphasis.

b Franz Kline. *King Oliver.* 1958. Oil on canvas, 8′3″ × 6′5½″ (2.51 × 2.1 m). Private Collection, New York. By permission of the Estate of Franz.

c Winslow Homer. *The Carnival.* 1877. Oil on canvas, 20 × 30″ (50.8 × 76.2 cm). Metropolitan Museum of Art, New York (Amelia B. Lazarus Fund 1922).

d Gustave Caillebotte. *Vue de Toits (Effet de Neige): Rooftops (Snow).* 1878. Oil on canvas, 25⅝ × 31⅞″ (65.1 × 81 cm). Musée d'Orsay, Paris.

d

a

b

c

Color and Balance

Unlike symmetrical balance, asymmetry is based on the concept of using differing objects on either side of the center axis. But to create visual balance, the objects must have equal weight or eye attraction. Color is often used to achieve this effect.

A comparison of **a** and **b** will illustrate the idea. In **a** Joan Miro's painting is shown just in black and white. From this reproduction, the composition might appear off balance. The left side, with the contrasting white circle and solid black triangle and notched rectangle, seems to have more visual interest than the right side, where there is less delineation of the shapes and little value contrast. But when the same painting is seen in color **(b)**, the balance is immediately clear. A circular shape on the right is actually a brilliant red in color. This very vivid color note in a predominantly neutral painting attracts our eye and can balance the elements on the left.

The use of color to balance a composition is very common and seen in many different periods and different styles of art. The formal, royal family portrait from the seventeenth century **(c)** is narrative and very naturalistic in style. But the balance is achieved in almost the same way as in Miro's nonobjective work **(b).** Here the left side has more figures and background details. But the brilliant red coat of the prince posed at the right provides the balance. Again, when this painting is seen just in black and white, the balance might not be clear.

The colors of the two buildings at the far right of Edward Hopper's painting **(d)** could hardly be termed brilliant or vivid. Yet in a painting dominated by greenish yellow and dull brown tones, they serve as color accents of balance. The large dark "hole" of the railway tunnel at the left is a strong element set against the light wall. The color of the righthand buildings (especially the dull orange) balances the high value contrast of the tunnel.

---

a Joan Miró. *The Birth of the World.* 1925. Oil on canvas, 8'2¾" × 6'6¾" (2.5 × 2.0 m). Collection, The Museum of Modern Art, New York (acquired through an anonymous fund, the Mr. and Mrs. Joseph Slifka and Armand G. Erpf funds and by gift of the artist).

b Seeing **a** in color shows us how color achieves the balance.

c N. Le Largillière. *Louis XIV and his Heirs.* Oil on canvas, 50¾ × 63¾" (129 × 162 cm). Reproduced by courtesy of the Trustees of The Wallace Collection, London.

d Edward Hopper. *Approaching a City.* 1946. Oil on canvas, 27 × 36" (68.58 × 91.44). The Phillips Collection, Washington, DC.

d

Color and Space

There is a direct relationship between color and a visual impression of depth, or pictorial space. Colors have an innate advancing or receding quality because of slight muscular reactions in our eyes as we focus on different colors. Intense, warm colors (red, orange, yellow) seem to come forward; cool colors (blue, green) seem to go back. The design of numbers in various colors (a) illustrates this principle. When we look at this design we can see that some numbers immediately "pop" forward and actually seem closer than others. Some numbers seem to stay back, with others seeming to be far in the background. Relative size can influence this effect, with larger items automatically seeming closer. But notice that size is not really a consideration here. There are numbers of equal size and weight that advance or recede based solely on their color.

Another aspect of the relationship of color and spatial illusion is that the dust in the earth's atmosphere breaks up the color rays from distant objects and makes them appear bluish. As objects recede, any brilliance of color becomes more neutral, finally seeming to be gray-blue.

Artists can use color's spatial properties to create either an illusion of depth or a flat, one-dimensional pattern. The landscape in **b** gives a feeling of great distance. The overlapping planes of trees and hills change in color and value. The artist has concentrated warm browns and oranges in the close foreground. Then, as distance increases, the elements become grayer, cooler, and more bluish in color.

In contrast, Bonnard in his landscape (c) consciously flattens and compresses space by his use of color. The foreground is in warm advancing reds and yellows, but now the background hills are a brilliant advancing orange that comes forward and denies the implicit depth of the scene. A colorful and decorative, but relatively flat, painting results.

Color values are also important in spatial illusion. Whatever the colors used, high contrast comes forward visually, whereas areas of lesser contrast generally recede. Examples **a** and **b** show this effect. The dark-colored numbers in **a** generally stay back, being close in value to the black background. The value-contrasting light yellows come forward. In **b** the far mountains are almost the same value as the light background sky. But the tree on the right side and the rest of the foreground contains dark, highly contrasting elements.

a Olivetti USA. Advertisement with Electric Calculator Symbols.
G. Pintori, Artist.
b Alfred Jacob Miller. *Rocky Mountain Scene, Wind River Mountains.* 1853.
Oil on canvas, 18 × 24″ (45.72 × 61 cm). J.N. Bartfield Galleries,
Inc., New York.
c Pierre Bonnard. *Mediterranean Coast.* Ca. 1923. Oil on canvas,
37¾ × 28½″ (96 × 72 cm). Phillips Family Collection.

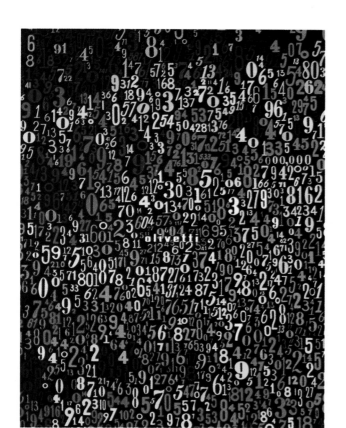

a

c

b

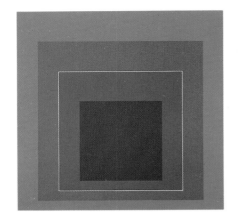

a

b

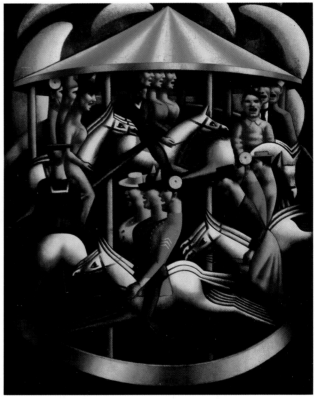

c

d

Color Schemes

MONOCHROMATIC, ANALOGOUS, COMPLEMENTARY, TRIADIC

There are four basic color schemes (or *color harmonies,* as they are often called).

A *monochromatic* color scheme involves the use of only one hue **(a).** The hue can vary in value, and pure black or white may be added. The visual effect is extremely harmonious and generally quiet, restful, and (depending on the range of values) subtle.

An *analogous* color scheme combines several hues that sit next to each other on the color wheel. Again, the hues may vary in value. The Japanese print in **b** shows the related, harmonious feeling that analogous color lends to a design.

A *complementary* color scheme, as the term implies, joins colors opposite each other on the color wheel. This combination will produce a lively, exciting pattern, especially with the colors at full intensity. The vibrant contrast of blue and orange plus the sharp dark and light changes make the *Merry-Go-Round* **(c)** a more dynamic and exciting visual pattern than **b.**

A *triadic* color scheme involves three hues equally spaced on the color wheel. Red, yellow, and blue would be the most common example **(d).** Because the hues come from different parts of the wheel, the result is contrasting and lively.

These color schemes are probably more applicable to such design areas as interiors, posters, and packaging than to painting.

In painting, color often is used intuitively, and many artists would reject the idea that they work by formula. But knowing these harmonies can help designers to consciously plan the visual effects they want a finished pattern to have. Moreover, color can easily provide a visual unity that might not be obvious in the initial pattern of shapes. Even though design aims vary, often the more complicated and "busy" is the pattern of shapes, the more useful will be a strict control of the color, and the reverse is also true.

Color unity is described by another term. We often speak of the *tonality* of a design or painting. *Tonality* refers to the dominance of a single color or the visual importance of a hue that seems to pervade the whole color structure despite the presence of other colors. Monochromatic patterns (as value studies in one color) give a uniform tonality, because only one hue is present. Analogous color schemes can also produce a dominant tonality, as **b** shows. When colors are chosen from one part of the color wheel, they will share one hue in common. In **b** yellow-green, blue-green, blue, and green all derive from the primary blue, so they yield a blue tonality.

a Josef Albers. *Homage to the Square: White Line Square 16.* 1966. Lithograph, 20¾" (53 cm) square. Collection, The Josef Albers Foundation.

b Hokusai. *Ryogoku Bridge at Evening from Ommayagashi* from *Thirty-Six Views of Fuji.* Color woodcut. Metropolitan Museum of Art, New York (Henry L. Phillips Collection, 1939).

c Mark Gertler. *Merry-Go-Round.* 1916. Oil on canvas, 74½ × 56" (189.3 × 142.2 cm). Tate Gallery, London. Reproduced by courtesy of the Trustees.

d Charles Demuth. *Buildings Abstraction, Lancaster.* 1931. Oil on board, 27⅞ × 23⅝" (71 × 60 cm). © The Detroit Institute of Arts (Founders Society purchase, General Membership Fund).

Color Discord

Color *discord* is the opposite of color harmony. A combination of discordant colors is visually disturbing, for the colors have no basic affinity for each other. They seem to clash, to pull away in opposing directions, rather than to relate harmoniously to one another. The term "discord" conveys an immediate negative impression. Discord in life, in a personal relationship, may certainly not be pleasant, but it often provides excitement. In the same manner, discord can be extremely useful in art and design.

Mild discord results in exciting, eye-catching color combinations. The world of fashion has exploited the idea to the point that mildly discordant combinations are almost commonplace. A discordant color note in a painting or design may contribute visual surprise and also may better express certain themes or ideas. A poster may attract attention by its startling colors.

Once rules were taught about just which color combinations were harmonious and which were definitely to be avoided because the colors did not "go together." A combination of pink and orange was unthinkable; even blue and green patterns were suspect. Today, these rules seem silly, and we approach color more freely, seeking unexpected combinations.

Colors widely separated on the color wheel (but *not* complements) are generally seen as discordant combinations. The following combinations will produce visual discord and are illustrated here.

Example **a** combines a primary and a tertiary that is beyond an adjacent secondary: red and blue-purple.

Example **b** combines a secondary and a tertiary beyond an adjacent primary: orange and yellow-green.

Example **c** combines two tertiaries on either side of a primary: blue-green and blue-purple.

In producing discord, value is an important consideration. As **d** shows, the impression of discord is much greater when the value of the two colors is similar. With great dark-and-light contrast between the hues, few color combinations will look truly unpleasant. But when the value contrast is absent, we begin to see the actual disharmony of the hues.

The painting by David Hockney **(e)** has many areas where purposely discordant color are placed together. Hence, the effect is visually exciting and unusual.

---

a Red and blue-purple.
b Orange and yellow-green.
c Blue-green and blue-purple.
d Pure orange and two shades of red-purple.
e David Hockney. *Nichols Canyon.* 1980. Acrylic on canvas, 84 × 60″ (213.36 × 152.4 cm). © David Hockney 1980.

a

b

c

d

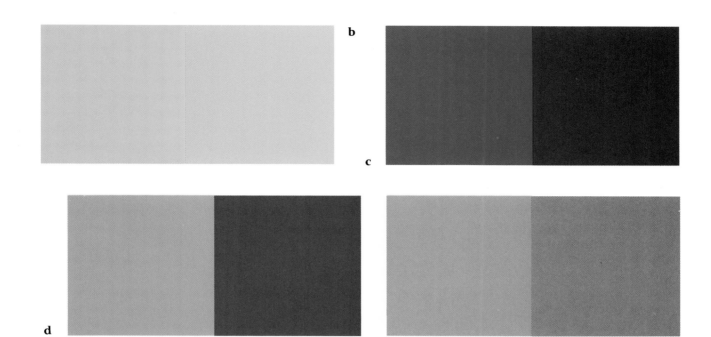

e

a

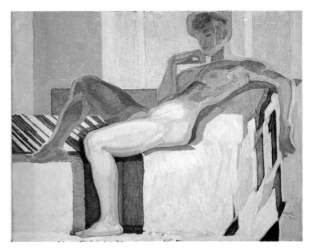

b

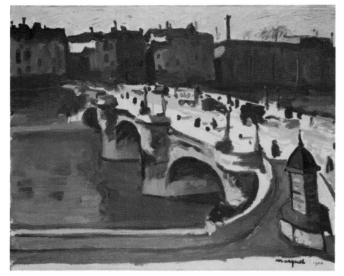

c

Color Uses

LOCAL, OPTICAL, ARBITRARY

There are three basic ways in which color can be used in painting. An artist may use what is called *local* color. This term refers to the identifying color of an object under ordinary daylight. Local color is the objective color that we ''know'' objects are: Grass is green, bananas are yellow, apples are red. The artist controls the color scheme mainly by the mental identification of the colors in the subject matter.

Visually, the red of an apple can change radically, depending on the illumination. Because color is a property of light, the color of any object changes at sunset, under moonlight, or by candlelight as in **a.** Even atmospheric effects can visually change the local color of distant objects such as faraway mountains appearing blue. An artist reproducing these visual effects is using *optical* color.

In *arbitrary* color, the color choices are subjective, rather than based on the colors seen in nature. The artist's colors are selected for design, aesthetic, or emotional reasons. The colors in Kupka's painting **(b)** were chosen for their spatial and decorative qualities, not for any objective reference to the natural colors of a nude woman. Arbitrary color is sometimes difficult to pinpoint because many painters take some artistic liberties in using color. Has the artist disregarded the colors he saw or has he merely intensified and exaggerated the visual reference? This latter use is termed *heightened* color. Albert Marquet's painting of Paris **(c)** is an example. Late on an overcast afternoon, the shadows in the city could well have a slightly blue or purple cast. Marquet has exaggerated, or heightened, this visual effect.

Pure arbitrary (or subjective) color is often seen in twentieth-century painting. Just as art in general has moved away from naturalism, so has arbitrary color tended to become an important interest. Even color photography—with filters, infrared film, and various darkroom techniques—has experimented widely in the area of unexpected color effects.

These categories of color use obviously apply to paintings with identifiable subject matter. In nonobjective art the forms have no apparent reference to natural objects, so that the color is also nonobjective. Purely aesthetic considerations determine the color choices.

---

a Georges de la Tour. *The Repentant Magdalen.* Ca. 1640. Oil on canvas, 44½ × 36½" (113 × 93 cm). National Gallery of Art, Washington, DC (Ailsa Mellon Bruce Fund).

b Frantisek Kupka. *Planes by Color, Large Nude.* 1909–1910. Oil on canvas, 4'11⅛" × 5'10⅛" (1.49 × 1.78 m). Solomon R. Guggenheim Museum, New York.

c Albert Marquet. *The Pont Neuf.* 1906. Oil on canvas, 19¾ × 24⅛" (50 × 61 cm). National Gallery of Art, Washington, DC (Chester Dale Collection).

Emotional Color

"Ever since our argument, I've been **blue.**"

"I saw **red** *when she lied to me."*

"You're certainly in a **black** *mood today."*

"I was **green** *with envy when I saw their new house."*

These statements are emotional. The speakers are expressing an emotional reaction, and somehow a color reference makes the meaning clearer, because color appeals to our emotions and feelings. For artists who wish to arouse an emotional response in the viewer, color is the most effective element. Even before we "read" the subject matter or identify the forms, the color creates an atmosphere to which we respond.

In a very basic instance, we commonly recognize so-called warm and cool colors. Yellows, oranges, and reds give us an instinctive feeling of warmth and evoke warm, happy, cheerful reactions. Cooler blues and greens are automatically associated with quieter, less outgoing feelings and can express melancholy **(a)** or depression. These are generalities, of course, for the combination of colors is vital, and the artist can also influence our reactions by the values and intensities of the colors selected.

Paintings in which color causes an emotional reaction and relates to the thematic subject matter are very common. But notice the difference that color *alone* can make in our emotional reaction to a painting. Examples **b** and **c** are nonobjective; there is *no* subject matter. Yet what a different feeling each work gives us because of the color choices. The reddish areas overlaid with foreboding heavy strokes of black in Soulages' *Peinture, 13 Fevrier 1960* **(b)** give an immediate dark, ominous emotional feeling without any subject reference. By contrast, the complementary blue and orange in Hofmann's painting **(c)** are vibrantly alive. These clean sparkling, bright colors give an instantly cheerful, pleasant effect.

It is interesting to note how the feeling of shape can be related to color. A jagged, angular, dynamic shape in a soft, grayish lavender can seem like a design contradiction. It is generally more satisfactory to select colors that relate to the emotional qualities already present in the shapes (or vice versa). All elements of a design should work together unless a deliberate incongruity (or visual confusion) is the desired effect.

---

a Pablo Picasso. *Two Women Seated at a Bar.* 1902. Oil on canvas, 31½″ × 36¼″ (80 × 92 cm). Private collection.

b Pierre Soulages. *Peinture, 13 Février 1960.* 1960. Oil on canvas, 3′8½″ × 4′9″ (1.13 × 1.45 m). Private collection.

c Hans Hofmann. *The Golden Wall.* 1961. Oil on canvas, 5′ × 6′½″ (1.51 × 1.82 m). © 1989 The Art Institute of Chicago (Mr. and Mrs. Frank G. Logan Prize Fund). All rights reserved.

a

b

c

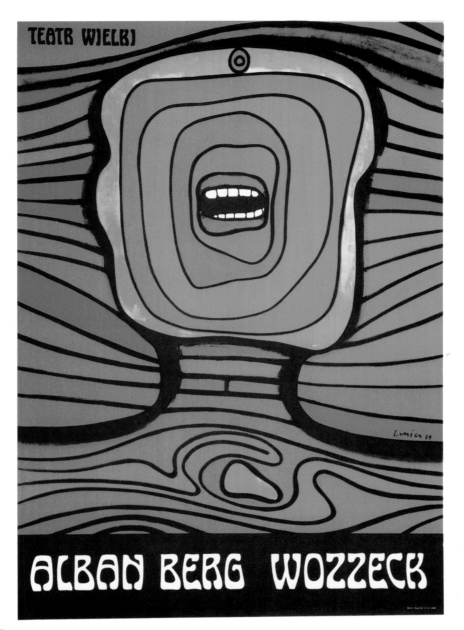

a

Color Symbolism

''Don't worry, he's true **blue.***''*

''I caught him **red***-handed.''*

''So I told her a little **white** *lie.''*

''Why not just admit you're too **yellow** *to do it?''*

We frequently utter statements that employ color references to describe character traits or human behavior. These color references are *symbolic*. The colors in the above statements symbolize abstract concepts or ideas: fidelity, sin, innocence, and cowardice. The colors do not stand for tangibles like fire, grass, water, or even sunlight. They represent mental, conceptual qualities. The colors chosen to symbolize various ideas are often arbitrary, or the initial reasons for their choice have become so deeply buried in history we no longer remember them. Can we really explain why green means ''go'' and red signifies ''stop''?

A main point to remember is that symbolic color references are cultural: They are not worldwide but vary from one society to another. What is the color of mourning that one associates with a funeral? In our society one would say black, but the answer would be white in India, violet in Turkey, brown in Ethiopia, and yellow in Burma. What is the color of royalty? We think of purple (dating back to the Egyptians), but the royal color was yellow in dynastic China and red in ancient Rome (a custom continued today in the cardinals' robes of the Catholic Church). What does a bride wear? White is our response, but yellow is the choice in Hindu India and red in China.

Different eras and different cultures invent different color symbols. The symbolic use of color was very important in ancient art for identifying specific figures or deities to an illiterate public. Not only the ancients used color in this manner—in the countless pictures of the Virgin Mary through centuries of Western art, she is almost always shown in a blue robe over a red or white dress.

Symbolic color designations are less important in art than they once were. Still, they linger on and can help an artist to create designs on specific themes. The dominant red-orange with discordant bits of red-purple in the poster in **a** symbolizes the opera's gruesome theme of insanity and murder as well as the composer's atonal music, with its lack of traditional musical harmony.

a Jan Lenica. *Alban Berg Wozzeck.* 1964. Offset lithograph, 38⅛ × 26½" (97 × 67 cm). Collection, The Museum of Modern Art, New York (anonymous gift).

Color Versus Value

We customarily think of an artist as working with color, but consider the vast area of drawings, woodcuts, etchings, and lithographs produced using pure value and no color. Also, consider fields such as sculpture and architecture. Here, though color is present, the main design consideration has often been value because of the usual monotone of the materials involved. Texture, which is so important an element in these fields, is essentially a variation in light and dark visual patterns. It would seem that an artist in almost any field or specialization should be skillful in manipulating both color and value.

Do color and value work together or at cross-purposes? This question has been argued over the centuries. Some critics have maintained that the emphasis in a work should be on one *or* the other. Some artists of the past seem to have thought this way also. Leonardo da Vinci called color the "greatest enemy of art," and Titian supposedly said that an artist needs only three colors. Obviously, these artists were content to rely on value changes, rather than contrast of pure color. The Fauves and Expressionists of the twentieth century would undoubtedly agree with Van Gogh's statement, "Coloring is what makes a painter a painter."

Historically, it seems that, for whatever reason, many artists have often chosen to put the emphasis on either color or value. Art historians outlining the stylistic changes in art have described shifts in this area as indicative of a new period.

If we cannot see a work of art firsthand, nothing gives us as faithful an impression of the original as a photograph in full color (even the paper color in a drawing adds to our pleasure and understanding). But black-and-white reproductions are a practical and economic necessity. This changing of color/value emphasis among different artists and different periods would explain why some works seem so inadequate when shown in a black-and-white illustration. A book on Impressionism, for example, without any illustrations in color would be impossible; it could barely hint at the sparkle and brilliance of the original paintings. The black-and-white reproduction of Bonnard's painting **(a)** is quite a drab interpretation of a work that when seen in color is rich and lush. But a Renaissance painting is satisfactory, if not satisfying, shown only in value. In twentieth-century art, Color Field painting loses its entire impetus when devoid of color; Super Realism can be appreciated without color, just as a black-and-white photograph *can* substitute for one in color.

It is doubtful that any instructor or critic today would ask artists to make a flat-out, definitive choice between color and value as the point of emphasis in their work. But it is intriguing that such a choice (conscious or intuitive) was apparently made by many great artists.

---

a Pierre Bonnard. *View from the Studio, Le Cannet.* 1945. Oil on canvas, 37½ × 49½" (95.25 × 125.73 cm). Milwaukee Art Center Collection (gift of Mr. and Mrs. Harry Lynde Bradley).

a

BIBLIOGRAPHY

GENERAL

Canaday, John. *What is Art?* New York: Alfred A. Knopf, 1980.

Dondis, Donis A. *A Primer of Visual Literacy.* Cambridge, MA: MIT Press, 1973.

Faulkner, Ray, Edwin Ziegfeld, and Howard Smagula. *Art Today,* 6th ed. New York: Holt, Rinehart and Winston, 1987.

Gilbert, Rita, and R. William McCarter. *Living with Art,* 2nd ed. New York: Alfred A. Knopf, 1988.

Preble, Duane, and Sarah Preble. *Artforms,* 4th ed. New York: Harper and Row, 1989.

ART HISTORY

Arnason, H.H. *History of Modern Art,* 2nd ed. Englewood Cliffs, NJ: Prentice-Hall, 1976.

Janson, H.W. *History of Art,* 2nd ed. New York: Prentice-Hall and Harry N. Abrams, Inc., 1977.

GENERAL DESIGN

Bevlin, Marjorie Elliott. *Design Through Discovery,* 3rd ed. New York: Holt, Rinehart and Winston, 1977.

Bothwell, Door, and Marlys Frey. *Notan: The Dark-Light Principle of Design.* New York: Van Nostrand Reinhold, 1976.

Collier, Graham. *Form, Space and Vision.* Englewood Cliffs, NJ: Prentice-Hall, 1967.

De Lucio-Meyer, J. *Visual Aesthetics.* New York: Harper and Row, 1974.

De Sausmarez, Maurice. *Basic Design: The Dynamics of Visual Form.* New York: Van Nostrand Reinhold, 1975.

Hoffman, Armin. *Graphic Design Manual.* New York: Van Nostrand Reinhold, 1977.

Hurlburt, Allen. *Layout: The Design of the Printed Page.* New York: Watson-Guptill, 1977.

————. *The Grid.* New York: Van Nostrand Reinhold, 1982.

————. *The Design Concept.* New York: Watson-Guptill, 1981.

Itten, Johannes. *Design and Form,* 2nd rev. ed. New York: Van Nostrand Reinhold, 1976.

Kepes, Gyorgy. *Language of Vision.* Chicago: Paul Theobald, 1969.

Kerlow, Isaac Victor, and Judson Rosebush. *Computer Graphics.* New York: Van Nostrand Reinhold, 1986.

Maier, Manfred. *Basic Principles of Design.* New York: Van Nostrand Reinhold, 1977.

Mante, Harald. *Photo Design: Picture Composition for Black and White Photography.* New York: Van Nostrand Reinhold, 1971.

McKim, Robert H. *Thinking Visually.* New York: Van Nostrand Reinhold, 1980.

Stoops, Jack, and Jerry Samuelson. *Design Dialogue.* Worcester, MA: Davis Publications, 1983.

Wilde, Richard. *Problems: Solutions.* New York: Van Nostrand Reinhold, 1986.

Wong, Wucius. *Principles of Two-Dimensional Design.* New York: Van Nostrand Reinhold, 1972.

————. *Principles of Three-Dimensional Design.* New York: Van Nostrand Reinhold, 1972.

VISUAL PERCEPTION

Arnheim, Rudolf. *Art and Visual Perception: A Psychology of the Creative Eye.* Berkeley: University of California Press, 1974.

Bloomer, Carolyn M. *Principles of Visual Perception.* New York: Van Nostrand Reinhold, 1976.

Ehrenzweig, Anton. *The Hidden Order of Art.* Berkeley: University of California Press, 1976.

Gombrich, E.H. *Art and Illusion: A Study in the Psychology of Pictorial Representation.* Princeton, NJ: Princeton University Press, 1961.

SPACE

Carraher, Ronald G., and Jacqueline B. Thurston. *Optical Illusions and the Visual Arts.* New York: Van Nostrand Reinhold, 1966.

Coulin, Claudius. *Step-by-Step Perspective Drawing: For Architects, Draftsmen and Designers.* New York: Van Nostrand Reinhold, 1971.

D'Amelio, Joseph. *Perspective Drawing Handbook.* New York: Leon Amiel, Publisher, 1964.

Doblin, Jay. *Perspective: A New System for Designers,* 11th ed. New York: Whitney Library of Design, 1976.

Ivins, William M. *On the Rationalization of Sight.* New York: Da Capo Press, 1973.

Luckiesh, M. *Visual Illusions: Their Causes, Characteristics and Applications.* New York: Dover Publications, 1965.

Montague, John. *Basic Perspective Drawing.* New York: Van Nostrand Reinhold, 1985.

Mulvey, Frank. *Graphic Perception of Space.* New York: Van Nostrand Reinhold, 1969.

O'Connor, Charles A., Jr. *Perspective Drawing and Applications.* Englewood Cliffs, NJ: Prentice-Hall, 1985.

White, J. *The Birth and Rebirth of Pictorial Space,* 2nd ed. New York: Harper and Row, 1973.

TEXTURE

Battersby, Marton. *Trompe-l'Oeil: The Eye Deceived.* New York: St. Martin's Press, 1974.

Proctor, Richard M. *The Principles of Pattern: For Craftsmen and Designers.* New York: Van Nostrand Reinhold, 1969.

Wescher, Herta. *Collage.* New York: Harry N. Abrams, 1968.

COLOR

Albers, Josef. *Interaction of Color,* rev. ed. New Haven, CT: Yale University Press, 1972.

Birren, Faber. *Creative Color: A Dynamic Approach for Artists and Designers.* New York: Van Nostrand Reinhold, 1961.

————, ed. *Itten: The Elements of Color.* New York: Van Nostrand Reinhold, 1970.

————, ed. *Munsell: A Grammar of Color.* New York: Van Nostrand Reinhold, 1969.

————. *Ostwald: The Color Primer.* New York: Van Nostrand Reinhold, 1969.

————. *Principles of Color.* New York: Van Nostrand Reinhold, 1969.

De Grandis, Luigina. *Theory and Use of Color.* Englewood Cliffs, NJ: Prentice-Hall, 1986.

Fabri, Frank. *Color: A Complete Guide for Artists.* New York: Watson-Guptill, 1967.

Gerritsen, Frank J. *Theory and Practice of Color.* New York: Van Nostrand Reinhold, 1974.

Itten, Johannes. *The Art of Color,* rev. ed. New York: Van Nostrand Reinhold, 1984.

Kippers, Harald. *Color: Origin, Systems, Uses.* New York: Van Nostrand Reinhold, 1973.

Rhode, Ogden N. *Modern Chromatics: The Student's Textbook of Color with Application to Art and Industry,* new ed. New York: Van Nostrand Reinhold, 1973.

Varley, Helen, editor. *Color.* Los Angeles: Knapp Press, 1980.

Verity, Enid. *Color Observed.* New York: Van Nostrand Reinhold, 1980.

INDEX

PHOTOGRAPHIC SOURCES

The author and publisher wish to thank the custodians of the works of art for supplying photographs and granting permission to use them. Photographers and sources for photographs other than those listed in the captions are given below:

A/AR: Alinari/Art Resource, New York
AR: Art Resource, New York
CG: Carmelo Guadagno
G/AR: Giraudon/Art Resource, New York
GC: Geoffrey Clements, Staten Island, New York
JA: Jorg P. Anders, Berlin
LCG: Leo Castelli Gallery, New York
PR: Photo Researchers, New York
RB: Rudolph Burckhardt
RM: Robert E. Mates
RMN: © Cliché Musées Nationaux/Service de Documentation Photographique de la Réunion des Musées Nationaux, Paris
S/AR: Scala/Art Resource, New York

Cover and title page (detail): ''Two Roses'', by David Holt, was originally created for David Holt Limited Editions, 1985.

Chapter 1 Opener: *Connections*, detail. 1986. Poster for Simpson Paper Co. James Cross, Art Director; Ken Parkhurst, Designer. Cross Associates. (3a) © 1983 John Kuchera.

Chapter 2 Opener: Wayne Thiebaud. *Pies, Pies, Pies*, detail. 1961. Oil on canvas, 20 × 30" (50.8 × 76.2 cm). © 1961 Paul Le-Baron Thiebaud. Crocker Art Museum, Sacramento, CA (gift of Philip L. Ehlert in memory of Dorothy Evelyn Ehlert). (16b) Courtesy Eugene Larkin. From *Design—The Search for Unity*, Wm. C. Brown, Publishers, 1988. (17c) Trustees of the late Barbara Hepworth, St. Ives, Cornwall, U.K. (21e) Amateur Athletic Foundation/LPI 1984. (22d) Ben Blackwell, Oakland, CA. (25b) Ferdinand Boesch/Pace Gallery, New York. (27d) RMN. (31c) Copyright Frequin-Photos. (32a) RM. (32b) Neg. 335877 (Photo by Logan), Courtesy Department of Library Services, American Museum of Natural History. (33c) A.F. Kersting, London. (35c) GC.

Chapter 3 Opener: John Steuart Curry. *Baptism in Kansas,* detail. 1928. Oil on canvas, 3'4" × 4'2" (1.02 × 1.27 m). Whitney Museum of American Art (gift of Gertrude Vanderbilt Whitney). (41a) David Stansburg. (45c) Annan, Edinburgh. (47c) © Bill Brandt/PR. (50c) Courtesy WGBH Educational Foundation, Boston.

Chapter 4 Opener: Mary Stevenson Cassatt. *At the Opera,* detail. 1880. Oil on canvas, 31½ × 25½" (80 × 65 cm). Courtesy Museum of Fine Arts, Boston (Charles Henry Hayden Fund). (59b) © 1983 Steve Rosenthal. (59c) Spanish National Tourist Office, New York. (60a) Joseph Szaszfai. (60b) A/AR. (63b) © 1988 Paul Warchol, New York. (63c) LCG. (74a) Svend Thomsen. (77c) LCG.

Chapter 5 Opener: Kent Twitchell. *The Holy Trinity with the Virgin*, detail. 1977–1978. Acrylic wall painting, 40 × 56' (12.2 × 17.1 m). Otis/Parsons Art Institute, Los Angeles. (81b) M. Knoedler & Co., Inc., New York. (81c) G/AR. (82a) A/AR. (82b) G/AR. (85a) Wolfgang Volz. (85b) GC. (85c) © 1986 Museum Associates, Los Angeles County Museum of Art. All rights reserved. (87b) A/AR. (90a) AR. (91b) Reinhard Friedrich, Berlin, West Germany. (91c) GC.

Chapter 6 Opener: Piet Mondrian. *Broadway Boogie-Woogie*, detail. 1942–1943. Oil on canvas, 4'2" × 4'2" (1.27 × 1.27 m). Collection, The Museum of Modern Art, New York (given anonymously). (96a) © 1976 Bruce Barnbaum. (99a) © ESTO/Ezra Stoller. (100d) Courtesy Terry Dintenfass Gallery, New York. (102b) © Copyright 1989 by Gruener Janura AG, Glarus, Switzerland. (103c) © 1981 Arizona Board of Regents, Center for Creative Photography.

Chapter 7 Opener: Roy Lichtenstein. *Nurse*, detail. 1964. Magna on canvas, 4' (1.22 m) square. Courtesy Leo Castelli Gallery. (109c) Norman McGrath. (113c) A/AR. (113e) Tass/Sovfoto, NY. (114b) RM. (114c) JA. (120a) Jim Strong, Inc. (120b) A/AR. (120c) LCG. (124c) JA.

Chapter 8 Opener: Juan Gris. *The Violin,* detail. 1916. Oil on wood panel, 45½ × 28½" (117 × 73 cm). Öffentliche Kunstsammlung, Basel. (128a) Courtesy Brod Gallery, London. (129b) G/AR. (131a) Photos by Bernd Kirtz. (131b) Rheinisches Bildarchiv Neg. No. 129338. (131c) GC. (132b) Musees de la Ville de Paris, © SPADEM 1989. (133d) GC. (135b) A/AR. (135c) Sov-Photo, New York. (136c) © 1981 L.A. Olympic Organizing Committee. (137d) Catalogue no. 33118, photo no. 83-10907, Dept. of Anthropology, Smithsonian Institution. (138a) GC. (139b) GC. (140b) The Granger Collection. (141d) RM. (143c) The Colour Company, Denver. (143d) Laurin McCracken. (145d) G/AR. (146a) GC.

Chapter 9 Opener: Lee Bontecou. *Untitled,* detail. 1964. Welded steel with canvas, 6' × 6'8" × 1'6" (1.83 × 2.03 × 0.45 m). Honolulu Academy of Arts. (148) RB/LCG. (151a) Bob Hanson. (151b) © ESTO/Ezra Stoller. (152a) G/AR. (155c) RB/LCG. (156a) Courtauld Institute of Art. (158a) Routhier/Studio Lourmel, Paris. (158b) Marilyn Levine/O.K. Harris Works of Art, NY. (158c) Rheinisches Bildachiv. (160a) Schumacher, New York.

Chapter 10 Opener: Gustave Caillebotte. *Le Pont de l'Europe,* detail. 1876. Oil on canvas, 49⅛ × 71⅛" (124.7 × 180.6 cm). Musée du Petit Palais, Geneva. (164a) Norman McGrath. (165b) CG. (168a) Philip Pocock. (171d) A/AR. (176a) Courtesy Richard Gray Gallery, Chicago. (179a) A/AR. (129c) H.G. Rauch. (184a) Photos by George Gardner. (185c) Soprintendenza per i Beni Artistici e Storici, Parma e Piacenza. (191d) Museum Moderner Kunst, Vienna. (191e) alt: Josef Albers. (192a) A/AR. (192c) Fotomas, Barcelona. (193d) GC. (195d) Helga Photo Studio. (197e) LCG.

Chapter 11 Opener: Bridget Riley. *Current,* detail. 1964. Synthetic polymer paint on composition board, 4'10⅜" × 4'10⅞" (1.48 × 1.50 m). Collection, The Museum of Modern Art, New York (Philip Johnson Fund). (203b) CG. (207d) A/AR. (208a) Magnum Photos, New York. (209d) CG. (209b) RMN.